Turning Ten

and other stories of life

Edited by
Claire Bell, Pete Court & Esther Cremona

Turning Ten and Other Stories of Life
Series number: 10

Compilation copyright © Claire Bell, Pete Court and Esther Cremona 2025. Copyright of individual chapters remains with the authors of those chapters.

All rights reserved. Other than for the purposes and subject to the conditions prescribed under the Copyright Act, no part of this publication may be reproduced, stored in a retrieval system, or transmitted in any form or by any means, electronic, mechanical, photocopying, recording or otherwise, without the prior permission of the publisher.

Cataloguing-in-Publication entry is available from the National Library of Australia http:/catalogue.nla.gov.au/.

This edition first published in Hackham, South Australia November 2025
Published in Australia by Immortalise via Ingram Spark
www.immortalise.com.au

ISBN 978-1-7638310-1-8

Typesetting by Ben Morton
Front cover design by Naw Day Day

Sponsors

We wish to thank the following organisations for their sponsorship of the Stories of Life creative writing competition and publishing venture:

Omega Writers
sponsoring the 2025 Stories of Life competition.

Immortalise
supporting the publication, sales and distribution of the 2025 anthology.

Tabor College of Higher Education
hosting the official launch of the 2025 anthology.

Foreword

Happy 10th Birthday to Stories of Life! Hip, hip, hooray!

Ten years ago, a bunch of story-loving Christian folk, involved in writing and publishing, asked people to share their stories of faith. The stories rolled in, and *Stories of Life* was born.

Every year, a diverse range of people submit their stories. It is always a joy to read how uniquely each of us experiences our faith in God. Stories told with humour, some with elements of grief, illness and ongoing challenges and several that champion humbling acts of humanity.

To those that have shared their stories across the past decade, we thank you. For those that are 'um'-ing and 'er'-ing about sharing stories of faith, we encourage you. We look forward to sharing so many more stories for the next decade.

God's gracious subtlety, in providing what we need, was evident for our cover story for 2025, titled *Turning Ten*.

Our feedback crew and editors for 2025 comprises Dr Pete Court, Claire Bell, Julia Archer and my good self. We are all on the same page when we say it is a fearsome responsibility and a great privilege to read each story submitted. The vulnerability and openness in these stories does not go unnoticed, and our team continues to learn and grow as humans, people of faith and literary professionals from reading your stories.

Thanks to Paula Vince for providing her expertise as proofreader extraordinaire. Paula is a respected award-winning author, who writes faith-inspired stories and books, along with fiction with an Australian twang.

A humongous shout-out to May-Kuan Lim, our fearless executive administrator, whose efficiency and humility is something to behold. To

Sponsors

We wish to thank the following organisations for their sponsorship of the Stories of Life creative writing competition and publishing venture:

Omega Writers
sponsoring the 2025 Stories of Life competition.

Immortalise
supporting the publication, sales and distribution of the 2025 anthology.

Tabor College of Higher Education
hosting the official launch of the 2025 anthology.

Foreword

Happy 10th Birthday to Stories of Life! Hip, hip, hooray!

Ten years ago, a bunch of story-loving Christian folk, involved in writing and publishing, asked people to share their stories of faith. The stories rolled in, and *Stories of Life* was born.

Every year, a diverse range of people submit their stories. It is always a joy to read how uniquely each of us experiences our faith in God. Stories told with humour, some with elements of grief, illness and ongoing challenges and several that champion humbling acts of humanity.

To those that have shared their stories across the past decade, we thank you. For those that are 'um'-ing and 'er'-ing about sharing stories of faith, we encourage you. We look forward to sharing so many more stories for the next decade.

God's gracious subtlety, in providing what we need, was evident for our cover story for 2025, titled *Turning Ten*.

Our feedback crew and editors for 2025 comprises Dr Pete Court, Claire Bell, Julia Archer and my good self. We are all on the same page when we say it is a fearsome responsibility and a great privilege to read each story submitted. The vulnerability and openness in these stories does not go unnoticed, and our team continues to learn and grow as humans, people of faith and literary professionals from reading your stories.

Thanks to Paula Vince for providing her expertise as proofreader extraordinaire. Paula is a respected award-winning author, who writes faith-inspired stories and books, along with fiction with an Australian twang.

A humongous shout-out to May-Kuan Lim, our fearless executive administrator, whose efficiency and humility is something to behold. To volunteer in this capacity for the last eight years is no small feat. As a published author herself, May-Kuan shows professionalism, thoughtfulness and leadership consistently. May-Kuan, we thank you.

We are grateful for the patience and enthusiasm of our cover design team for 2025, combining the talents of Ben Morton, May-Kuan Lim and Naw Day Day.

Our judges for the 2025 anthology are published authors, devoted to the glorious beauty of great storytelling. The judge for our short stories category is Dr James Cooper, a founding member of *Stories of Life*, and Head of Creative Writing & Communication at Tabor College.

The judge for our open stories category is Catch Tilly, a published author with a passion for reading and writing and a powerful imagination. Catch is a legend of Young Adult literature.

Both judges feel blessed with being able to read the varied range of stories in both open and short categories.

Stories of Life is supported by you – the contributors and the readers of this anthology. Since 2021, the cash prizes have been covered by entry fees and book sales. This has been possible because all *Stories of Life* committee members are volunteers. We are also resourced in kind by Omega Writers, Tabor College and our esteemed publication service provider, Immortalise.

Connection to others, finding hope and marvelling at the wonder of God's creation are threads of light that shine across all stories. Thank you to the writers who have submitted stories this year. If you are reading this and pondering 'Should I send in a story?', the answer is yes.

Everyone has a story to tell.

Blessings

Esther Cremona

The Judges

James Cooper is a South Australian writer and teacher of writing at Adelaide's Tabor College. His work has appeared in numerous journals including *Quadrant*, *Light Quarterly*, *Dappled Things* and *An Unexpected Journal*. In 2024 he was awarded the Max Fatchen Fellowship as part of the South Australian Literary Awards, and in 2022 his debut novel, *Something about Alaska*, was published by MidnightSun. For more information please visit his website: jacooperwrites.com

Catch Tilly describes herself as a dual citizen of Australia and imaginary worlds. She has five children, two degrees (including an MA in Creative Writing from Tabor) and a husband of 30 years. She has worked as a teacher, actor, scriptwriter and features editor. Her novel *Otherwise Known as Pig* was published by Wakefield in 2019, a confronting look at bullying with a surprising Christian twist. Catch is currently working on Book Three of the *Shadowalker* series, an apocalyptic story of dragons, laser swords and a girl who walks through death.

Catch says, 'Stories are the way we connect to the world and how we step past ours and others' prejudices into truth and empathy. To be part of bringing stories of faith to the world is a glory and a privilege. Thank you for your courage and faith in submitting them and letting me into your story.'

Contents

Foreword iv

The Judges vi

Mother Duck 1
    Chris Lee

Is it Safe? 3
    Roslyn Bradshaw

Veronica 6
    Jeanette Woods

Dizzy Spell 11
    Vera Hardiman

Quandong Birthday 16
    June Hopkins

Our Numbers 20
    Clara Johnson

Even Here 24
    Caitlin Pywell

The Kindness of Strangers 26
    Julia Archer

My Little Ray of Sunshine 31
    Liisa Grace

Turning Ten 36
    Jenny Woolsey

Cursed by Her Mother 41
    R J Rodda

One Hundred NOT Ninety-Nine 43
    Lesley Beth Manuel

Steering True 46
    Chris Lee

A Ghost of an Idea 51
    Rory O'Donnell

A Journey through the Shadows 56
    Sandy S Lish

Birthday Cake Faith 62
  Natalie Ingram

To the End of their Days 64
  Lynda Worrell

A Whisper Away 69
  June Hopkins

Chosen 71
  Carolyn Tonkin

Redhead 77
  Roslyn Bradshaw

God's Light in the Darkness 82
  Hazel Barker

Saying Goodbye to Faith 84
  Elizabeth D Guntrip

Fragile 87
  Kezia Pettitt

Nan, What Took You So Long? 89
  Raewyn Elsegood

Babies are Still Dangerous 92
  E Taylor

Another Ordinary Day 95
  Karen Roper

When Despair for the World Grows in Me 98
  Tamara Harpford

An 'Ordinary' Faith 100
  Lexia G Mackin

Happy Caterpillar Smiles 105
  Diana Davison

Blowing Balloons May be Hazardous to Your Health 107
  Anusha Atukorala

A House for Fay 109
  Jo Wanmer

Seeing the Sparkle through Tears 111
  Karen Curran

Crying Help 114
    Phil Bell

Wheels of Change 116
    Jo Wanmer

'But That's a Cult…' 121
    R J Rodda

An Unrelenting Love 125
    Brock Meier

Blowing my Mind 128
    Adah Christabel

A Lost Child Before Being Found 133
    Yen Daly

The Graces of Dawn 139
    Rory O'Donnell

Out of the Shadows 141
    Kylie Gardiner

Rodrigo 146
    Barbara McKay

The Lion 152
    Simone Field

Mother Duck
Chris Lee

I am 'crazy duck lady'.

My husband has chooks which I'm not too fussed about and our three adolescent children are too tangled in screens and surging hormones, stumbling about learning how to navigate a crazy world, to pay much attention elsewhere; but I love my ducks.

Watching them swim about on the dam is a balm to my soul. It's a calm and quiet world where sleek heads dip and shimmer, wings stretch and water glitters, where something in me exhales.

My bantam girl 'Kansas' is my favourite. Her olive beak is unique. White feathers are peppered with freckles of grey across her wings, and a treasure of shiny emerald green hides on the underside.

She'd recently hatched nine perfect ducklings, and my heart soared. Tiny golden buttons bobbing on the surface like dandelion wishes. But the dam is perilous for such little nuggets, with ravenous crows and hawks flying overhead. I had to get them to a safer space. I had plans.

I found myself waist-deep in the cold water, hammering star pickets into the mud and rolling out chicken wire so they had an enclosed haven with their mum for a short period as they grew.

The problem was, those tiny little baubles could still fit through the chicken wire. As I enclosed Kansas in her new house, the little ones scooted sporadically into the wider dam, happily swimming around, obliviously launching at bugs while Kansas darted and flapped from behind the wire, quacking frantically for them to stay close, her cries desperate: 'Get back here! It's not safe out there.'

My still, small voice did not achieve much, though I tried to reassure. 'Kansas! It's okay. I see everything from here. This is for their protection, I won't let anything happen to them. Even while they're straying, if something flies overhead, I have my big stick as defence. Nothing stands a chance against me. Be patient, trust me, I'm bringing them back to you!'

As I stood there in that water, closing up the holes and using my rod to gently direct the little ducklings back to their mum, I felt the quiet voice of revelation whispering to my spirit.

I am Kansas.

I've been flapping and fussing at God about my children: trying to make sense of what's going on, anxious for the future I can't see, about what they're getting into, choices they're making that might not be particularly wise, the distance they're straying.

But there stands God. Providing, protecting, comforting; loving us. Rod and staff in hand, securing our perimeter, aware of the dangers that circle overhead.

Poor Kansas in such turmoil, not knowing I have this under control. It's going to be okay. I'm standing right there in that cold muddy water with her – and with her precious ones. I love them too. I am gently guiding them home.

Poor Kansas. Poor me. We panic in the unknown. But from where God stands, he can see everything. We're going to be okay.

Is it Safe?

Roslyn Bradshaw

I had thought about this trip for a long time. My aunt worked there for years as a missionary nurse, and I wanted her to write about it, but when she died, all I had were her slides and letters. Writing the tale was up to me, but as the book took shape, I felt God urging me to go.

'Where are you going?' my friend asked.

'Ethiopia.'

'Is it safe?'

'I've checked the Smart Traveller website, and the civil war is in the north, in the red zone. The southern highlands, where she worked, are in the yellow zone.'

'Does that mean safe?'

'Um. White is safe. Yellow means "Consider your need to travel."'

'And?' She raised her eyebrows.

'Well, it's been twelve years since she passed. Soon, there won't be anyone alive who knew her. That's the point of going: interviewing people and experiencing the place. The mountains. The roads. The scenery.'

Someone suggested booking a tour and adding a side trip to see my informants. I discovered that most Ethiopian tours had been cancelled due to unrest. One company could arrange customised safaris, so I booked a Land Cruiser and a driver, who would meet my husband and me in Arba Minch and drive us down south. Then there were the multiple vaccinations and health warnings to consider.

One night, lying awake, I felt panic rising. *Am I crazy? No, I will trust God. He said, 'Go.' I'm going.*

At the Addis Ababa hotel: metal detectors, armed guards. At the airport: disorder, jostling, unfamiliarity. Short packed flight. Arba Minch: narrow airstrip flanked by eucalypts. Relief. A smiling man holds a sign with my name.

Belet, our driver, was friendly, fluent in English and knowledgeable about Ethiopia. Plus he drove carefully. Our journey through the rift valley wound past palms, settlements and isolated huts. Occasionally, enthusiastic children mobbed our vehicle to hawk mangoes and avocados. Every few kilometres, shepherds herded goats and hump-backed cattle off the road to let us pass. Belet pointed out the colourfully dressed people walking on verges, carrying Bibles, using floral umbrellas to shelter from the sun.

'It's Sunday. They are going home from church.'

As that first day unfolded, a sense of calm slowly seeped into my soul.

Each day brought fresh revelations.

At Sawla, a resident called Elias said, 'This area is now 85 per cent Christian.' Referring to the time of the previous government, he said, 'Our fathers spent a lot of time in prison.'

At Waka, one woman recounted, 'Because of your aunt, our babies now live.'

Another chimed in, 'If Miss Longmire touched you, you were 90 per cent sure of being healed.'

An old man said, 'Before she opened the clinic, she prayed. She told about Jesus.'

'Did many believe then?'

'If not, then later. After a week. A year. They never forgot her touch, her love.'

I was moved to tears. Impacted. Despite difficulties, dysentery, mountain sickness and scarce amenities, God's peace buttressed me throughout our Ethiopia trip.

I felt safe.

Veronica

Jeanette Woods

Fifty years ago, we hadn't been married long. Life was beautiful, we had both graduated from Bible College and were looking forward to discovering what God had ahead for us. We expected that it would be cross-cultural work in an Asian country, but knew we needed to get used to being married first.

We were very involved in our local church; Peter was a lay reader and we had started a Kids' Club and a youth group as well.

One day our pastor called us and said that a girls' hostel had asked if there were activities for young people because they had a teenager who wanted to attend. That was how we met Veronica. She was seventeen, tall, friendly and a little awkward socially. She had some developmental delay, probably because of her disadvantaged background. Her mum died with three-month-old Veronica in her arms, and her father was alcoholic, so she had become a ward of the state.

We didn't know much about her, but she won our hearts and before long was staying with us often and became part of our life. She was talkative and funny, and sometimes I wanted a break from her when I came home from my teaching job. We related well over cooking; she loved to bake, especially to eat what she had made!

Veronica was a teenager, but in some ways still a child. So she enjoyed youth events but felt most at home in the kids' club. Soon she became our assistant, helping with games, craft and setting up, and was very keen to go on the camps we ran. Everyone loved her and the church became her family and the place where she belonged.

Veronica

As our relationship strengthened, we had a niggling worry. By this time, we had been accepted to go as missionaries to Indonesia and would be moving to Melbourne to train. Veronica could not come with us, and we did not want her to feel abandoned again, so we asked our minister and his wife and his family to care for her.

The other big news was that we were expecting our first baby, and Veronica felt like it was her sibling. We left Adelaide with a few weeks to go before the birth, making plans for her to visit us later when our little girl was born. Veronica bought her train ticket to come and stay with us after Christmas.

There was a disturbing phone call on Christmas Eve to say that Veronica seemed to have disappeared and might not be on the train to Melbourne. That was hard to believe, so Peter went to meet it and waited at the station until the last person had gone. Veronica was not there.

Where could she be? We knew she had been counting the hours to come to us and would not have missed that train. The police, however, saw it differently, and reassured everyone that she was a teenage runaway and would turn up. We knew something bad had happened.

Our lives moved on – there was nothing more we could do for Veronica at that point – and we went to Indonesia, finally arriving in Papua, where our work began. There was a long silence regarding Veronica.

In April 1978, sixteen months after she disappeared, we received news that Veronica's body had been found in the bush near Truro, north of Adelaide.

Our young friend was dead and probably had been since before the day that Peter looked for her on the train. Although we always felt that something had happened to her, the reality was shocking and made me feel physically ill. We sat on the edge of the bed and sobbed in disbelieving grief. We would never see Veronica again. We held each other as our emotions poured out until we were spent, and then I looked up at the bedroom wall.

There was a fabric banner – a precious memento made for us by the church children when we left Adelaide. Right at the top, was Veronica's message. 'The Lord is my Shepherd. I shall not want. Psalm 23:1'. We hugged each other tightly and felt a peace creep in and sit next to our sadness as we remembered that she knew the Good Shepherd and was safe. She was one of the world's nobodies, yet in God's eyes she was a precious lamb. We both knew in that moment the supernatural comfort of God's grace and love.

The police thought she had got lost and died of thirst, but you can see the Sturt Highway from the spot Veronica was found, and it made no sense. Still nothing happened.

It would be another year before the scale of the tragedy unfolded, revealing the loss of seven girls in what has become known as the infamous Truro murders. It was a sordid, shocking story that we put behind us, knowing that there were six other extended families who were plunged into grief as their lives changed forever.

In the days before the internet, we were not even aware of how it all unfolded. We had moved on with our lives, had three children of our own and one we had lost.

Fast forward forty years. I was in hospital recovering from surgery. Bored, in pain and not sleeping. After chatting with a night nurse who had written a book about losing her mother, I literally heard a voice say, 'Write about Veronica'.

Veronica

How could I? I knew almost nothing, let alone so long after. But it niggled me and I began searching the internet. Thus began my journey of giving her a voice and declaring that her short life was valuable to God. That night I began to write.

Eventually Peter and I drove to Adelaide to follow up leads, and to retrace Veronica's movements. We visited her unkempt grave and vowed to fix it up and make a new plaque, which we did.

Over the next months I tracked down the police commander who headed up the investigation when the police had finally paid attention.

I found the parole officer who signed off on the perpetrator's behaviour that gained him early parole and had been haunted by that ever since.

I found the court artist who drew the sketches that go in the newspapers reporting the trial.

Through an amazing coincidence I found the mounted policeman who headed up part of the massive search in the Truro bush. No-one had ever heard the details he was able to describe.

We walked through the city to the bus stop where Veronica accepted a ride and was never seen again. We knew by then that she had been shopping that night to buy presents for us and our baby, and clothes for her trip.

Best of all, in the last hours of our Adelaide trip, through the Salvo Missing Persons organisation, we found the matron of the girls' hostel from which Veronica disappeared. We heard first-hand what happened that night. For the first time we discovered that this beautiful lady had advocated for Veronica and pestered the police, and been present in court. We had some very long hugs.

All that was left after that was to make the pilgrimage we had planned to the Truro bush. But the lady who found the matron for us was very pastoral and stopped us in our tracks. She said two things: 'You are still grieving, aren't you?' and 'Have you forgiven those men yet?' For the first time in this project, I cried.

I knew that the sadness had been buried for forty years. Through my project, it was emerging again, rearing its head and triggering memories. I didn't want to even say their names or give any airtime to those two men. This project was about Veronica. I knew at that moment that pushing away pain and sadness for forty years does not deal with the root of it. I knew God's forgiveness in my life. I even knew that God could forgive the worst criminal. But could I forgive these men too?

At the lawn cemetery, the murderer's plaque said: 'Beloved son and brother. Untold love and joy he brought to all.' I realised that even his family were victims in this crime. We were all co-victims.

We spoke our truth, pain and anger out aloud, and then spoke forgiveness in Jesus' name. It was incredibly liberating.

Even though I was dreading it, we drove to Truro and set up the plaque and planted a shrub and felt amazing peace. Peter and I began to see that the whole journey of the book was for us as much as Veronica. As we headed home, a beautiful rainbow formed an arch over the road – God's promise of hope. We drove into it for another two hours and felt blessed.

These things remain: Veronica is safe with Jesus, her story has been captured forever, and our hearts are at peace until we are reunited in eternity.

Dizzy Spell
Vera Hardiman

In the days before mobiles,
I had a debilitating dizzy spell that
derailed me.
I was in my thirties, a new believer
in Jesus, with young children to collect from school.

The dizzy spell comes suddenly.

I stop driving and get out of the car.
My head is spinning.
I'm too sick to drive.

I vomit on the bonnet.

Maybe now I will feel better and
be able to drive?
I ask myself.
I get back into the car.
My head spins.
Now I feel sick again.

Oh God, help. Help me, God. Oh, God, I feel so sick,

I call out to my Lord.
I get out of the car yet again and
I am sick on the bonnet
again.

Yet again, I climb back into the car.
My head is still spinning.
Maybe I can try driving now?
I again ask myself.

No, I can't drive yet.
I don't feel better.
I call out to my Lord,

I can't believe this. What am I going to do?
How do I call my husband for help?
Should I knock on someone's front door?
Ask to use their phone?

I have no answer from my Lord.
I tell myself how silly I am:
Good idea, Princess, but you are forgetting something.
You are forgetting that you can't walk.
Your head is spinning.

Dizzy Spell

I pray,

Oh, help me, God. I am desperate, and I need you.

Help me, Jesus.

A man appears

at my driver's side window.

I ask myself,

Is he a friend? Or is he a foe?

I don't know.

I decide to take the risk.

I open the window.

He is holding a strange-looking long device.

I cannot work out what it is.

I frantically ask myself again,

Is he friend or foe?

I think I answer:

Friend.

I don't think he wishes me harm.

He says:

I can call any number you need. I work for Telecom.

I repeat his reassuring words to myself.

I can call any number you need. I work for Telecom.

For a moment, I am lost for words.

Then I think about God.

How does he do this?

I ask myself.

I explain to the Telecom man what has happened and what I need.

He is very matter of fact.

He does not plague me with questions.

He does just what I ask.

He calls my husband and tells him where to come and why.

Before leaving, he rings the school and tells them what has happened.

No questions asked.

Thank you,

I whisper.

Thank you, God! You are amazing!

My peace returns.

I relax.

I wait.

My husband appears. All is well.

They say God sends angels

Dizzy Spell

to help his little flock.

Later that day, my husband takes me to the doctor.

Diagnosis: Labyrinthitis.

Here are tablets to stop the vomiting.

The doctor is helpful and kind.

Thank you, Jesus.

To the kind stranger:

So tirelessly you telephoned.

You have been a trustworthy and

tender-hearted Telecom technician. Thank you

Quandong Birthday

June Hopkins

Anxiety etched itself on my mother's face; however, my father's unperturbed demeanour had the bigger impact on my siblings and me. If he refused to be anxious also, then we were certain everything would be alright, provided that the rain stopped soon.

Dad had acquired a job on an outback property which could take him away from the family for several months. My mother agreed to withdraw my three siblings and myself from school to accompany him to the job. We would have correspondence lessons for the duration, possibly six months. An old, rather tumbledown cottage on the property was available for us to use. It was situated a couple of kilometres along a rutted track from the main homestead, wherein the property owner and his rather haughty wife lived their lives quite separate to the workers.

We had barely arrived and hadn't settled in at the cottage when unseasonably heavy rain began. The novelty of our new circumstances disappeared in the puddles that surrounded the cottage and, unfortunately, in many spots indoors. Water dripped through holes in the roof, keeping us busy continuously emptying strategically placed buckets, pots, and pans.

Rain pelted down non-stop for ten days, and then intermittently for another three weeks. It could be up to two months before the road to and from the property was fit for purpose. The mail truck, which also brought our perishable food supplies and school lessons once a week, did not come for fear of becoming stuck for weeks in the clingy, black-soil mud. Even the track from our cottage to the homestead was impassable, being so muddy it would take hold of tyres or feet with a vice-like grip. We were effectively on our own.

Quandong Birthday

My mother attempted to keep us all entertained in between emptying the various water-filled receptacles. She played memory word games with us: *'I went shopping and I bought a loaf of bread...I went shopping and I bought a loaf of bread and a new hat...I went shopping and...'* We sang songs and recited poetry we'd learned in school. We put on impromptu plays, tickled each other, fought with each other, and watched the endless rain tumbling down. Dorothea Mackellar's poem about Australia being a land of droughts and flooding rain proved thoroughly accurate. We certainly heard the drumming of an army as the steady soaking rain was relentless.

Dad was probably bored but I thought he was enjoying his slow down. For once, he took time to tell us stories from his boyhood, surprising us with different voices as he described memorable characters. We were enabled to get to know our father a little better in those rain-soaked weeks. I like to think he enjoyed us a little more then, too. We loved hearing his tales.

Mum had brought enough food to last us about three weeks, but with not much else to occupy us, we'd consumed almost everything in two. The anxiety which grew on my mother's face made me wonder if we were going to starve to death. Still, she worked wonders, creating unique meals to which she gave made-up names. 'Yumbolinis' were scraps of spam pocketed in balls of flour and fried. Eventually, Mum confided that apart from a small quantity of sugar and flour, there was so little food remaining it would take a miracle of some sort to keep us being fed.

I was worried because I was about to turn six and it seemed there would be no party and no present for me.

Gathering us together to say our evening prayers, my mother declared she was going to stop worrying and start relying on God to provide for us.

'I'm going to ask God to give us this day our daily bread,' she stated, sounding a bit happier. I quietly added 'and something for my birthday, please God.'

The next morning the sun came out, hot and bright, and shone for most of the day, reviving our flagging spirits. In the late afternoon my parents suggested we take a walk while we could, as the ground had dried out a little. We were overjoyed, so we cheerfully slipped, slid, and skipped where we could with Dad and Mum into an area of the surrounding bush. After twenty minutes or so, we stopped in front of a small tree with droopy foliage, laden with large glossy-red, berry-like fruit.

'That's a quandong tree,' my father explained. He told us that Aboriginal people had valued it and used it in their diet for aeons.

'Can we eat the fruit too?' I asked.

'Yes, but the berries are a bit sour, so the fruit tastes best if it's stewed with some added sugar.'

We all helped pick the fruit. Dad took off his hat and we filled it with the berries, then Mum made a sack from her apron, and we filled that and our pockets also.

'I think God has answered our prayers,' Mum said, examining the quandongs when we reached the cottage. After sitting on the front step to scrape the sticky mud from our shoes with a stick, we eagerly went inside to see what Mum would make from the fruit. We helped peel the flesh from the seed inside each berry. With the remnants of our sugar and flour, Mum baked a quandong pie, saying it would be for my birthday. With juice squeezed from the remaining fruit, and added sugar, we also had cordial for a birthday party the following morning.

Quandong Birthday

While I slept, Mum and Dad created a game of Chinese checkers for my gift, using the large, round, wrinkly, ball-like seeds from the quandongs. They used charcoal to colour half of the seeds black and an antiseptic solution, Mercurochrome, to paint the rest a bright red. For the time being the game would be played on a checkerboard constructed from the side of a cardboard box.

Bright sunshine and a cloudless sky greeted my birthday morning. There were smiles all round, with an almost tangible feeling of hope and light-heartedness. We sat to enjoy a 'breakfast birthday party.'

The pie filling was a little tart as was the cordial, but we didn't care. We ate and drank with enthusiasm.

It was a memorable birthday. After we feasted on the pie and enjoyed the cordial, I was given the gift. I exclaimed, 'God answered my prayer too.'

Thankfully the rain had gone. The station owner managed to traverse the track from his house to our cottage, and came bearing gifts of rice, powdered milk, eggs, flour, and sugar – enough to ward off impending starvation. The ground dried over the next week or two and everything gradually returned to normal. Quandongs had taught me that God hears and answers our prayers.

Our Numbers
Clara Johnson

My husband loves numbers. So do I. In fact, he loves them so much that he studied them at university. So did I. These were our numbers: 6 – the number of years that we had been married, 2 – the number of girls that we were doing our best to raise, 1 – the number of babies growing inside me. Definitely just 1, we'd checked.

This story begins 2 days before Christmas…

Back in those days, 20 was a magic number. Before 20, you could. After 20, you couldn't.

20 what? 20 weeks.

That was almost how long I had been carrying my baby girl. For just under 20 weeks, she had been growing. 19 weeks and 3 days, the sonographer calculated when we saw her, the scan pushed forward by a few days due to Christmas shut downs.

Ultrasound is one of the most amazing inventions when you're pregnant. It's the closest thing to taking your baby's first photo. Lying on that bed, looking at a screen as they found her 5 fingers all curled up and her little foot pushing out, all I could do was marvel. I had started to feel little flutters, but seeing the image of her little body just blew me away, every time. Her perfect little heart beat was like a rhythm that made my heart beat all the faster. I could see the fingerprints of God all over her little body. He was slowly, carefully knitting her together, cell by cell. She was tiny and beautiful and ours.

Our Numbers

The sonographer pressed buttons that made the image change from black and white outlines to golden shapes – 2 little arms and 2 little legs, that moved as she poked and prodded at my belly. The technician typed letters as she took measurements that didn't really mean a lot to me. Flashes of red and blue flickered across the screen. I didn't pay them much attention. I was just enjoying the images of this little person whom I wouldn't get to hold for many more months yet. As our appointment neared its end, the technician told us that there had been one concern.

'One measurement – her nose bridge. It's considered a marker for Down Syndrome. Do you want to terminate?'

'No.'

'20 weeks is the cut-off.'

'That's okay. We're not going to.'

'You should make an appointment to see your doctor.'

Back in the car, it took less than 3 seconds for my husband and I to agree that terminating – we didn't even want to think about what that word meant – wasn't a consideration. There were just 2 days until Christmas and there were just 2 people we told that day about the technician's concern. The weight of the load that we felt we were carrying that Christmas was about 1 tonne. It rested on our shoulders through every carol we sang and every joyful gathering we attended. Just a few short days after Christmas, we would reach their magic 20. And it was on that day that we saw the doctor again.

We sat, my husband and I, in her office, as she explained to us what it meant to have a soft marker. The doctor explained to us that our numbers had changed. The chances of us having a child with Down Syndrome had just increased dramatically.

'Would you consider termination?'

'No.'

'Have you considered the effect on your family?'

She offered to fudge the numbers, give us an extra couple of days to run more tests, before we reached an adjusted magic 20. We shook our heads. We asked our questions. And we went home, trying to work out how our child's life had just become a question of numbers, probabilities, risk factors and chance.

Down Syndrome?
Trisomy 21?
3 copies of the 21st chromosome?

I created a new list of numbers. They were printed on a piece of paper, tucked inside my hospital bag. Phone numbers and websites for support services, in case we needed help with feeding or caring for a baby with Down Syndrome. I had one additional ultrasound to check that she didn't have Down Syndrome-related heart issues. And we praised God that she didn't. It felt like my husband and I had a thousand conversations about decisions that we needed to consider if we were going to be raising a child with additional needs. But all the time we told very few people. We didn't know how to talk about our numbers, but we loved talking about our new, growing family member.

Our Numbers

For 38 weeks, I carried my baby girl. The day she was born was a blur, as most of childbirth usually is. I could only marvel at the Creator who would design our bodies to go through this process to bring about new life. She was a beautiful bundle and as she lay on my chest for the first time, with her perfect little nose, I thanked God for her. After months of speculation, we could see for ourselves that she didn't have Down Syndrome. Not that it mattered. We loved her, just because she was our little girl.

Our numbers had changed: 3 busy girls, 2 'no's, 1 growing family, 0 regrets.

Even Here

Caitlin Pywell

'Don't fall asleep yet, stay awake,' I tell myself as I sit through another class at school, trying to make it to the last bell.

At sixteen years old, I was a high achiever – a swimmer, a piano player, a sister and a friend. Until one day, I wasn't.

A viral infection – unrelenting fatigue, brain fog/confusion, muscle weakness, migraines and pain. Visits to the doctor resulted in nothing. No answers, only more questions.

Imagine facing test after test, seeing doctor after doctor, to get the same answer – 'You're very sick but we don't know what with, so we can't do anything about it'…for eight long years.

I don't have to imagine it; this was suddenly, unexpectedly, my reality. Until one day, a specialist who had come across my condition before was able to do accurate testing and, finally, I received my first diagnosis. Naively perhaps, I thought, 'This is it, it's got a name, now let's fix it.' Unfortunately I was wrong…my specialist told me there's no cure, only ways to manage the pain, but it doesn't always work. And it didn't stop there. This condition came alongside another five conditions, each with their own set of challenges.

'God, where are you in this mess?' I cry myself to sleep wondering why. Knowing that I need to hold fast to my faith, for without it there is no hope. I trial many available treatments, trying to find the best combination, whilst also learning to live with these disabling conditions.

Even Here

Fifteen years into this journey and sometimes I'm still asking why. 'Why do I live with a disability? Why haven't I been healed this side of heaven?' I may not know all the answers, but I do know that God's not finished writing my story. He's been with me the whole time and will continue to be with me every step of the way. He cries when I cry and comforts me in the darkness and loneliness. His presence is always near. Even here.

The Kindness of Strangers

Julia Archer

When I was eight months pregnant with our first child, my husband suggested we go caving.

In the Papua New Guinea Highlands.

'It's a chance for you to get out of the heat and humidity here in Port Moresby. It's lovely up there in Kundiawa. I've been told Chimbu Lodge even has an open log fire in the evenings.'

His old caving friends from university were flying up to explore the Chimbu caves. He wanted to join them, and a weekend's reprieve from Moresby's heat...well, for me that would be heavenly. But...*caving?*

'You don't actually have to go to the caves, just fly up with us,' he said.

Well, okay. I could sit by the windows of Chimbu Lodge and look out at mountain scenery while the guys went off to clamber through their caves.

I'd be absent from church on the Sunday morning, but, really, I attended mainly from habit and for the social contact. I brushed away that little problem.

I just hope the baby doesn't decide to come early. Port Moresby hospital wasn't great, that was true, but it would surely beat any medical care in a remote small town.

Below our little high-wing plane, the landscape was green baize draped over sharp objects. Some of those sharp objects passed us uncomfortably close.

The Kindness of Strangers

Then we were flying over a rumpled green valley towards a flat-topped hill in the centre. A runway bisected a small town of scattered buildings. Below each end of the runway the hill fell steeply to the valley floor.

The pilot put us down perfectly, we taxied to the little terminus building, and one of the Lodge staff was waiting to collect us in a blue Land Rover.

As the only woman in the group, I was directed to the front passenger seat. The four Australian men climbed into the back, under the beige canvas cover.

The Lodge was a long, two-storey building, brick and concrete, with rooms looking out over a tropical front garden and the valley and mountains. We got ourselves settled, and I could imagine spending tomorrow very pleasantly, sitting on my private balcony looking at the view, resting a book on my growing baby.

And that evening there was, indeed, a log fire at the end of the lounge room, and a nice, if somewhat basic, dinner.

On Sunday morning, there seemed to be a change of plan.

'Why don't you at least come on the drive?' my husband suggested. 'You don't have to go down to the caves. You could sit in the Land Rover and just enjoy the view. Bring your book. We'll only be a couple of hours.'

I looked at him and his friends, standing there in the early sun. Their mountain-trekking long legs. None of them could imagine my perspective on this.

Ever unwilling to be seen as the timid little woman, I climbed back into the front seat.

The road out to the caves was unsealed red clay, constructed by pick and shovel and wheelbarrow. The Land Rover was built for this. I was not. The baby bounced up and down painfully on my pelvis. I grabbed the bar on the dashboard and lifted myself slightly off the seat. I rode the rest of the way like a Melbourne Cup jockey.

Finally, to my relief, we arrived. Not that this hillside spot was any different to any other point along the road. Only the local driver, who was now to become the tour guide to the caves, would have known where to stop.

We all got out. The men in shorts and boots. Me in a summer dress, sandals, and my handbag over my arm like the Queen.

The caves, apparently, were at the bottom of the hill. The cavers had to walk down through a local village's sweet potato field, then follow a stream to the mouth of the caves.

'Would you like to come with us and at least see the caves from the outside?'

No, I did not want to go, but nor did I want to embarrass my husband in front of his friends by arguing.

We slithered down the hill, the deep red soil sliding away under our feet. My sandals filled with dirt. After a few minutes I stopped and looked back up to the road. It seemed so far away.

I shouted after the others, now way below, 'I think I won't go down there. I'll just sit in the Land Rover until you come back.'

'Are you sure you'll be all right?' my husband called up to me. 'Do you want me to come back and sit with you?'

Seriously? Having come this far, how could I ask him to let his friends go on without him?

'No, I'll be fine. Honestly.'

So they continued sliding on down the hill, doing heaven knew what damage to the sweet potato field, and I turned around to go up.

And I couldn't move. My feet went up and down on the same spot. Every step slid back to where it started. I was totally stuck. Stranded. And alone.

From out of nowhere, a dozen local children appeared on the road above, and stopped dead. A foreign woman, visibly pregnant, in a dress, with a handbag on her arm, standing in their vegetable garden.

They came rushing down, bare feet not slithering or sliding at all, and two or three on either side seized my arms and almost levitated me back up to the road, my feet hardly touching the ground.

They stood around discussing this for a few minutes, before vanishing just as suddenly as they had appeared.

The kindness of strangers.

The front of the Land Rover was locked. I clambered into the back, under the beige canvas cover. My book was also locked in the front, so I stared out across the scruffy landscape of hills and valleys, forest patches and vegetable gardens, and a few hillside villages. The many shades of green slowly becoming blue with distance.

After a while I had a feeling I wasn't alone. I peeped out from under the cover, and a local woman was sitting on the embankment above the road, watching me, chewing betel. When she saw my face she smiled, showing teeth blackened or missing from a lifetime of betel use.

Startled, I ducked back out of sight.

When I checked again, she was still there, still chewing, still smiling, watching over this poor stray foreign women who'd apparently been abandoned.

And who might, by the look of her, need a midwife any minute.

And so we sat for the next two hours.

Yes, the kindness of strangers, towards a totally vulnerable foreign woman who had wandered into their world.

For sure, I had skipped church with hardly a thought, but God was with me there on that remote hillside, taking care of me all the same.

The baby? He arrived just after his due date, and was perfectly fine. He's fifty-six this year.

My Little Ray of Sunshine

Liisa Grace

Was it her?

I peered through the window, my heart pounding. A familiar car had pulled up in front of the neighbour's house, and I squinted to see if it was my daughter.

I hadn't seen her in many weeks. She's forty now, but she's still my baby, my firstborn – and I knew she was living in her car, lost in the fog of addiction.

Despite my constant messages of love and open invitations to come and stay with us, she always refused. Instead, she slept underneath the bright lights of service stations, dark side streets, or somewhere along the beach, facing the ocean. Occasionally, she was calling late at night, terrified that someone was stalking her.

On that warm autumn day, I watched as she emptied her car onto the street – bags, clothes, blankets tossed over the footpath, the bonnet and roof of her car.

I felt torn. I longed to run out and hold her, but I stayed inside praying for her safety.

Then just as suddenly as she'd arrived, she loaded her things back into the car and drove off. I felt guilty for not going to her. Had I missed my chance?

A few hours later, she returned, parking in the same spot in front of our neighbour's house. She stayed in her car, curled up on the front seat, sleeping or maybe just exhausted. I left her, knowing she might not have slept for days.

As the sun dipped below the horizon, I walked out and gently touched her arm through the open window. Her skin was hot and clammy, her words incoherent. 'Mum, I feel like I'm dying,' she moaned.

I managed to get her inside, gave her medication, made up a bed, and watched her through the night. Her body ached, her temperature was low, yet she felt sticky and hot to touch. I prayed hard – prayers of desperation.

By morning, her condition had worsened. I pleaded with her to let me take her to the hospital. She finally agreed, and we inched our way to the car. She collapsed into the back seat, barely conscious.

At the emergency entrance, nurses wheeled her straight in, without her stirring as she slept throughout the entire process.

My mind flashed back to the day I left the hospital with her in my arms, just seven days old, when a song came on the radio – *A Little Ray of Sunshine* – dedicated to her.

The diagnosis was alarming: Golden Staph, sepsis, and a severe bone infection. I later found out the likely cause – a used needle prick, not from using, she insisted, but from the many used needles in her car. It didn't matter. The infection was real, and it was trying to kill her. In the first two days, I thought she was slipping away; I had to hold her eyelids open so the doctor could see her pupils.

For three weeks, she remained in hospital. When she was discharged, I booked us an Airbnb to allow her to recover and maybe hit the reset button.

A week later, her health spiralled downhill again, and she was admitted for another three weeks.

My Little Ray of Sunshine

Her moods swung like a pendulum. One moment she'd be talking non-stop for hours, coming up with elaborate plans; next, she'd be sleeping so much from being sedated that she'd eat in her sleep. She entered the hospital underweight, but devoured food like she hadn't eaten in months.

Still, she found joy in unexpected places, befriending other patients and lifting spirits wherever she sensed sadness. She pranced down corridors, unconcerned with rules or appearances. As her sister once said, she is a force of nature.

I was with her constantly. When I wasn't working, I was by her bedside. My fear, my guilt – they chained me to her. I didn't know from one day to the next what I would walk into. I was unravelling inside, trying to hold everything together.

My little ray of sunshine. She ignores social norms and believes that rules are meant to be bent. Nor does she believe in lids or pegs, convinced they are both restrictive. Bottles spill. Clothes fall off the line. 'If they land there,' she says, 'that's where they belong.'

She was diagnosed with bipolar disorder twenty years ago after surviving a suicide attempt. Now we also suspect ADHD. Labels aside, she's bold, unpredictable, and unique. Her personality is larger than life; once you've met her, you will never forget her.

I recently described her as a hurricane, but more accurately, a tornado, upturning things everywhere she goes. I say this with warmth and humour.

After six weeks in hospital and an additional two weeks with me, she left. Once her car was working again, she was gone in a flash, craving freedom, chasing something she couldn't name.

Turning Ten and other stories of life

For two weeks, she disappeared. A few scattered texts. A voice recording here and there. Every night, I checked my phone a dozen times. I feared police knocking on the door with the news no mother wants to hear.

I desperately clung to my hope and faith in God. I prayed fervent, raw prayers. But unlike before, the fire inside me had dimmed. I still believed in God, but I felt abandoned and isolated, like maybe this was how our story was meant to unfold. I went to see my pastor. I spoke to a psychologist. Still, I felt like I was losing my mind – misplacing keys, zoning out, forgetting what I was doing or where I was going. It became difficult to function.

'God, where are you? I feel like I'm drowning, please…help.'

My baby girl, my firstborn child, had been battling meth addiction, and after four years of it, she finally admitted it. When I look into her eyes, I can see the internal war raging inside her.

One day after another psychologist appointment, I snapped. I got in the car and drove, determined to find her. I scoured the area where I suspected she would be. I searched for hours. Finally, I saw her car. Doors flung open, boot jammed, and all of her belongings scattered everywhere like a scene from a movie I never wanted to watch.

She spotted me and skipped over. 'I knew I'd see you today, my mama,' she chimed. I tried to look her in the eyes, to call out the chaos, but she deflected, shifting the conversation, angry and agitated. I drove away, hot tears rolling down my face, struggling to breathe, my heart splitting into pieces.

My Little Ray of Sunshine

The next day, I returned to my pastor and his wife. I asked them to pray for our situation as I wept. I was hyperventilating, unable to get my words out as I finally let go of the fear, the guilt, and the illusion of control.

As I left their office, I felt something I hadn't in months: peace.

The very next day, while picking up my grandson from school, I tripped over a concrete bollard and fell to the ground. I struggled to get up, but my foot was badly damaged. I tried standing numerous times, but the pain was unbearable.

Initially, I kept telling my grandson that I would hold onto him as I hopped into the car, but that was the adrenaline talking.

After x-rays and scans, the diagnosis was clear: a rare complex mid-foot fracture, bony avulsion, and plantar 1st and 2nd metatarsal fractures. I knew this meant I would be off my feet for many weeks.

And the strangest thing? I felt incredibly grateful; for the forced rest, the interruption and the stillness.

Just a few weeks earlier, I was drowning in despair, spiralling with fear. Now, with a broken foot and my world on pause, I was breathing normally again. Hope was stirring. Not because the situation had magically resolved, but because I had finally surrendered.

I let go and let God.

Turning Ten

Jenny Woolsey

8 August, 1977

'Happy Birthday to you. Happy Birthday, dear Jenny. Happy Birthday to you,' sang the smiling nurses and the young patients seated around two long tables.

'Let's give ten claps for Jenny!' Matron exclaimed, bringing her hands together.

I smiled as I surveyed the kaleidoscope of exuberant children, all with bandages or plaster casts, eagerly awaiting their party food. The nurses, including Matron, stood beside the seated children, wearing their stark uniform of starched white dresses

'Now, who would like a piece of cake?' Matron asked.

'Me, me, me, me,' the golden-haired boy beside me chanted. Other hands went up.

Sister sliced the cake with its swirls of buttercream icing, placed generous pieces on small plates and circulated them. A knot formed in my gut as I watched each child receive some of my cake. My eyes grew dark as the little girl with pigtails across from me shoved the entire piece of cake into her mouth. Blobs of icing smeared across her lips like the Joker's smile.

Nurse Maria pushed a tumbler, holding a bubbly drink with a bent straw, towards me. 'Jenny, would you like some lemonade?'

Tears filled my eyes, overflowing down onto my cheeks. I scrunched my fists, shook my head, and stood up, knocking my wooden chair over. I didn't pick it up. Instead, I stomped back to my hospital bed, climbed onto the sterile, crisp white sheets and lay on my side. There was no cake for me. There were no treats for me.

This was the worst birthday ever!

Last day of Year 5, Semester One, 1977

'Please, Mr Staveley, can I have my report card now, as I'm going into hospital?' I said as my class sat cross-legged on the blue carpet.

I waited, wanting to escape for the holidays. Each name was called – Sharon…Keith…Joanne…Bradley. Soon no one sat around me.

'Jenny.' Mr Staveley handed me my report card. 'I wish you all the best for your operation.' His eyes showed warmth. 'I will be in touch with Mum to know how you're going.'

I nodded. So much for being first out!

During the holidays, preparations were made. The shopping list included new, pretty cotton nighties, undies, colouring and puzzle books, novels and colouring pencils. I was going to be in the hospital for about six weeks.

'This is also for you,' Mum said, holding out a small, round, black wrapped item. On the paper a Spanish lady swished her red frilly dress. She held a fancy fan. I unwrapped the item. It was soap. Immediately, I held the cake of soap to my nose and inhaled. My nostrils filled with the divine fragrances of citrus, lavender, spice and wood.

In early July, on the day of my admittance, I walked up the cold concrete stairs to the stone-clad Mater Children's Hospital in Brisbane. I'd never been inside the hospital before, and butterflies flapped in my tummy. I tightened my grip on Dad's hand.

Inside the ward, I shivered as I saw two rows of baby- and child-sized cots. A desk with a pile of folders, where a nurse sat writing, was at the end.

After being welcomed by the matron, I was shown to my bed, and I climbed in. Mum and Dad stayed for a while, then kissed me and turned to leave.

'Please don't go!' I begged them. Fear consumed me like a wildfire. 'Please, I don't want to stay here.'

Dad bent to give me another hug and I clung to him.

'We can't stay,' Dad whispered into my ear. 'You will be okay. We'll come tomorrow after work.'

Tears streamed down my cheeks as Mum and Dad left.

I lay on my hard bed with its ironed sheets and stared up at the ceiling. Maybe I could imagine I was at home in my bedroom, under my crinkled sheets that smelt like floral washing powder, surrounded by my favourite dolls. I cuddled Coco, my stuffed dog, tight to my chest.

Inside my tummy, a feeling started. Panic filled me. I needed to wee. The nurses were attending to other children and I couldn't call out. The pain grew so intense that I began to cry again.

'What's wrong, Jenny?' a kind female voice said.

'I-I-I need to go to the toilet,' I stammered.

'I'm Nurse Charlotte,' she said. 'Let's get you out of your bed so you can go.'

'Jenny, dear, how are you feeling today?'

A lady with an Irish accent, dressed in a nun's habit, smiled at me. Her eyes sparkled and her smile radiated warmth.

Turning Ten

'Scared.' I cuddled Coco to my chest again.

'I understand, it is scary having a big operation on your face,' Sister Angela Mary said, patting my arm. 'I have something for you.'

She handed me an envelope which I opened with curiosity. It contained a handcrafted holy card, made from embroidered silk, trimmed with ribbon. I ran my fingers over its shape – a curved hexagon. In the middle, Mary and boy Jesus prayed. A bouquet of dainty blue flowers finished off the keepsake. It was beautiful.

'God will be with you during your operation. He will look after you.'

'Thank you,' I said, and propped it on my bedside table, beside the 'Jesus loves you' card I had received from my Sunday School.

The surgery for my craniofacial deformity, Crouzon syndrome, was performed on July 22nd.

This surgery was the first of its kind in Queensland. Groundbreaking. Ten hours under the knife. My eye sockets, facial bones and maxilla were moved forwards, fused and built up with rib and hip bone grafts. Afterwards, my jaws were wired together and I could only 'drink' my meals, hence why I couldn't eat any birthday treats and was offered the lemonade.

There were complications, and my optic nerves became swollen, leading to blindness in my left eye and loss of three-quarters of the peripheral vision in my right. The surgery was extremely traumatic and my physical recovery took months. My emotional recovery took years. I returned to school towards the end of the year with my 'new' face.

As one could imagine, this was a highly stressful time for Mum and Dad, who had my two brothers at home to care for, worked, and visited me each day. St. Andrew's Presbyterian, my family's church, was a huge support.

Mum often speaks about Maris, who sat with them the day of my surgery and continually prayed for our family, Father Francis from St. Michael's The Abbey, who prayed and regularly asked after me and invited Mum and Dad to a special dinner, and the Sisters of Mercy at the Mater Hospital who were friendly, warm and loving. These people showed love in action and my parents were so appreciative.

That beautiful, embroidered silk card I received from Sister Angela Mary Doyle RSM AO forty-eight years ago is propped up in my display cabinet. It reminds me to never underestimate the power of sharing something that represents the love of Jesus to a child. Before the surgery, in the weird-smelling ward, on my own, with unfamiliar people and crying children, I was very frightened…but that holy keepsake and the 'Jesus loves you' card gave me immeasurable comfort.

I may not have enjoyed my tenth birthday party, but that afternoon Mum and Dad and my brothers arrived with bags full of presents and cards from many people, and letters from my classmates. I smiled and drank my tumbler of lemonade.

'Happy Birthday to you. Happy Birthday, dear Jenny. Happy Birthday to you,' sang my family.

'Ten claps,' my brother Steven squealed, bringing his hands together.

Cursed by Her Mother
R J Rodda

Beneath the circus sign on a dilapidated building, a huddled figure dressed in drab, dirty clothes buried their face in a plastic bag, shaking it back and forth. My companion, a young lady from Uzbekistan called Yasmina, stopped.

'Let's talk to her,' she said.

I would have walked on by. Beggars are a familiar enough sight in the city of Batumi on the Black Sea that draws millions of tourists in summer, attracted by the ubiquitous casinos and pebbly beaches. I might give money to them, but I never stopped.

We approached the person, hesitating before the shoes that marked her territory, and tried to connect using the national language of Georgian. No response. The head remained inside the bag, shaking it. A passerby told us, 'She only speaks Russian.' That made sense. The beggars were usually Russian-speaking foreigners, not the local Georgians, who took good care of their own.

Yasmina called out again, this time in Russian, which she is fluent in. The plastic bag still shook, but then suddenly the head popped up revealing an old lady with a sweet, lined face, grey hair and minimal teeth. Her name was Elizabet. She was very interested to hear Yasmina speak and tell her about Jesus. She also took the bananas I happened to be carrying, although with less enthusiasm. The old lady told us of her dark past, how she had been cursed by her mother, how God didn't love people like her.

Turning Ten and other stories of life

Yasmina and I disagreed with this. We took Elizabet's grimy hands and prayed with her. While Yasmina spoke in Russian, my eyes drifted beside the old lady and latched onto the alcohol bottle at her side, mostly full with a dark red liquid.

After prayer, the lady spoke of her desire to drink. We talked some more and went to a mini-mart nearby to get her some food to eat since she obviously was not keen on bananas. We got the fritz she asked for and some pita bread to eat it in. Yasmina also bought antiseptic hand wipes, passing one to me to use and taking one for herself. Then she took one to wipe clean the hands of Elizabet before handing her food. Elizabet looked incredulous as if she could not believe the food was for her.

Afterwards Yasmina took her hand and sang her a song in Russian about Jesus, me chiming in when it came to the easy parts.

We left her, and my companion commented how much Elizabet had stank but how God had helped her cope with it. I'd had a blocked nose and hadn't smelled anything. I was remembering Elizabet's interested, incredulous gaze and how I wouldn't have ever considered stopping.

One Hundred NOT Ninety-Nine

Lesley Beth Manuel

My mum was always a little vain, but we loved her. My sister and I found out our cousins had always called her 'Queenie'. Two years older than Queen Elizabeth II, Mum followed her life and dressed in similar style – often complete with pearls!

'Would have been Mum's 100th birthday today!' I messaged my sister.

I smiled at her return text, 'One of the roses on her rose bush opened today. Feels like a cheerful *hello* from Mum.'

A few years earlier, Dad had put up his hand to say he could no longer manage Mum's dementia. Miraculously, two rooms became available in the beautiful, new nursing home across the lane from their retirement village unit. Two rooms at the same time? Rare!

We were pleased Mum and Dad took the rooms. Miraculously, their request to take their queen-size bed was accepted. With a view of the sea, one room became their bedroom and the other a sitting room.

Close to Mum's 99th birthday, my sister asked, 'Someone's birthday is coming up. How old will you be?'

Mum's eyes lit up, 'One hundred!'

My sister and I both raised our eyebrows, looking at each other. Did she really believe that? Or was it a temporary memory mix up? We decided to ask another time. Same answer!

Maybe that's what happens when you hide your age for years?

We laughed. Growing up, Mum never revealed her age. Turned out she was older than Dad. Now she wanted to be a year older. Or was she holding out for a message from the Queen?

Mum was deteriorating. We joined in a family agreement to pray for our wish for Mum and Dad to leave this world together. Dad's preference was always for Mum to go first so she wouldn't feel abandoned.

We planned Mum's One Hundredth Party, and pre-warned everyone to go along with her significant birthday.

Receiving all the attention, Mum was in her element – until one kind resident who'd missed the memo approached. She had gone to the effort of finding two number 9 stickers to make a Happy 99th Birthday card. Mum took one look at the card and shook it in front of Dad with disdain. Apart from that, we partied without betraying the misconception.

Events thereafter unfolded out of our control – but not out of God's. Not long after her big birthday bash, Mum became bedbound. A few days later, Dad fell and broke his hip.

Wheeled to the ambulance bound for hospital, Dad frowned firm instructions, 'Take care of Gwen!'

We had two options for Dad: to become bedridden, or a 'not great option at 97' hip replacement. Horrible decision, but a life in bed was unbefitting for a man who had been active and adventurous all his days.

During the operation, Dad had a stroke and woke with a dead right side, and inability to talk or swallow. He now had to be fed with a tube.

Together or alternately, my sister and I visited Dad in hospital or Mum fading fast in the nursing home.

Others joined us praying that somehow Dad would get back to Mum in time, and that they would be together soon in eternity.

One Hundred NOT Ninety-Nine

Dad pulled out his feeding tube. The decision was made to return him for palliative care to his Gwen. Side by side on beds pressed together, Dad held Mum's hand all night. Her hand still in his, Mum passed next morning.

Between sorrowful visits with our dying Dad, we arranged Mum's funeral five days before Christmas – after that, things would be closed till New Year.

The minister Mum had chosen was unable to come from another state, so we contacted the minister from the last church they'd attended. He met us at the nursing home and turned out to be more than perfect! He was willing to conduct a joint burial and memorial service should Dad pass soon. Respectfully, he knelt beside Dad's bed, held Dad's hand and prayed.

The funeral home could arrange a double gravesite burial – but only if they had the signed death certificate by Friday, or it would have to be postponed for the holidays. Dad died on Thursday – six days after Mum. We thanked God for his gracious kindness.

I'd chosen a song to play as our parents were lowered into their graves side by side. The final triumphant lyrics of 'What a Day that Will Be' faded at the exact time the minister began his final prayer. God's perfect timing once again.

Steering True

Chris Lee

Ukulele: check. Soft toys: check. Reading material: check. Schedule – out the window: check. Anxiety…sigh…check.

Life on the road, even for a limited time, was a dream come true. We'd been planning our long service leave trip across the top of Australia since the kids were young, and the intermittent processes of preparation served to steadily fuel the passion for such an extended trip. The ultimate plan had whispered to us through the years and now finally its voice was loud and present. We were ready. The exhilaration was unmatched, but the dreaded companion that had come to haunt me over the years would not be left behind.

Our kids were aged 10,12 and 14, the perfect ages to take in the adventure that lay ahead. We set off in our old, brown 80's pop-top caravan to head through every state, with primary plans of free camping, desert tracks and isolated bush. It would turn out to be over 20,000 kms with over 5,000 of those on dirt roads.

I was prayerful as we left, not only for travelling mercies, but in thankfulness: for my family, my extremely capable husband David, God's beauty in creation and the opportunity to see this amazing country.

The feeling of quiet excitement, like an inflated balloon bobbing in the breeze, hovered tenuously above the threat that coiled closer and closer, ready to strike and pop it, and end its wild dance.

Anxiety.

It was an enemy that had subtly worked its way into my inner circle. I had opened the door at times. Often unaware, I let it overstay and it took full advantage, growing and claiming ownership of my body, thoughts and emotions. This trip was fertile ground for its eruption, with new experiences and unknowns around every corner.

As I prayed through the different scenarios that would arise, aware of my tight chest and racing thoughts, God's grace allowed one thought to dominate them all: 'Goodness and mercy.' Surely goodness and mercy were the prevailing blessings, following me all the way. The words were playing on repeat in my mind, even as I came up against situations that threatened to deflate my paper-thin balloon.

The first crack in the surface came when our caravan suspension broke on the Oodnadatta Track in 40°C heat. The claws of anxiety slashed viciously and a wave of panic erupted like fault lines in fragile ground. Stuck in the middle of nowhere, with no help in sight. Yet the quiet whisper from the distance continued…

'Goodness and mercy…'

We managed to limp to Coward Springs where my resourceful husband was able to 'tie' the van together with the original telegraph wire that had been spread across the country 100 years ago, and the kids plucked a tune on the ukulele aptly titled 'Oodnadatta Track'. Little delights like these were fighting a tug-of-war in my embattled mind. We dawdled the next 1,000 kilometres to Alice Springs where we were able to get some welding done and be ready for the rutty Tanami Track. All the while, my teeth were gritted in desperate prayer, trying to manage anxiety-driven headaches and stomach cramps as my enemy continued to flash its sharp talons at my sensitive joy, threatening to tear it apart.

'Goodness and mercy…'

'Goodness and mercy…'

As we hit the unfamiliar realm of croc country, every time the kids poked their toes in some water, anxiety would seize my soul, emphatically insisting it alone deserved my focus. Sometimes it was hard to enjoy the beauty and blessing that surrounded.

At one point we found we had naively been waist-deep, fishing in a shore break at Broome that was known for both salties AND sharks, and at Derby, I swore I saw ripples under the water that were speedily making their way towards us before we decided to get off the low-lying jetty.

'Goodness and mercy…'

From slippery roads to the unknowns of croc country, to dubious river crossings, despite the pleasures in every day, anxiety always wanted to take the lead. The crux came for me in Lawn Hill National Park, Queensland, where the fast-flowing, narrow causeway we were to tackle the next day robbed me of both peace and sleep. I was sure we would slip over the edge. Were there still crocs in this area? What if we couldn't get the kids out of the sinking car? I had never been so stressed in my life and even as I prayed, my body only heard the shouts of anxiety and responded in waves of churning sickness and throbbing dread. To make matters worse, the ranger happened along, nonchalantly proclaiming, 'Yes! Cars DO go over the causeway all the time!' It was enough for the ever-present enemy to deal the death blow. Even David told the kids to take off their seatbelts and wind their windows down – prepared for the worst-case scenario.

My mind was reeling but I somehow managed to precariously cross the tumultuous stream and stood waiting on the other side to video the scene, all the while acting as though I was not about to go into heart failure. I stood waiting, and desperately praying, 'God, no matter what happens, I know you're good.'

Steering True

As David edged forward my prayers turned to guttural pleas: 'Oh GOD! Oh GOD!' as the caravan wheel slipped off the causeway. That moment felt like an eternity as I waited for the rest of the van to follow and pull the car with it. The crumbling inside my soul engulfed me as I held my breath and felt the tears rise. My family inside the car were oblivious as, in reality, it only took a second for David's careful steering to pull it back onto the concrete and then they were across and pulling up next to me with water dripping all around the van.

'Goodness and mercy...'

'Goodness and mercy...'

I was in speechless shock as we drove on. I looked back at the kids. They sat with smiles and chattered to each other, flicking through books and activities that were part of their occupation for the trip. They were oblivious to the monster that had been tormenting me. The back seat was clear, there was no suffocating haunting, nothing to squash their joy or steal their excitement.

I turned back to the road. The red sandy, sunburnt country, rocky outcrops and glowing flora, drew me back...

'Goodness and mercy...'

I breathed in deeply as I looked at David navigating the current sand and ruts, and suddenly the realisation hit me. How it was that those children could have such an attitude; how they could sit back and enjoy the whole adventure, even with the same circumstances and possibilities I was facing.

They trusted the driver.

They knew *he* knew where he was going and how to get there. They knew that he knew how to drive – that he was the best one to be at the wheel. They knew there was no cause for worry, as long as their dad was driving. *He* was in control and they could just sit back and enjoy the ride. Sure, there'd be danger at times, sure there were potholes and ruts, but he'd give them instructions when needed. He'd tell them to hold on and he'd bring them through.

I turned my inward eyes towards *my* driver as I glanced in awe at the wide-open expanse of outback Australia and the clear vaulted sky above. Suddenly anxiety tucked its tail between its legs in defeat and fled in terror.

The words of truth echoed in my mind: The Lord is my Shepherd…I lack nothing…He leads me beside still waters…He restores my soul…I will fear no evil for your rod and staff comfort me…My cup overflows.

My cup was overflowing.

What a blessing it was to take that trip, travel sandy tracks, swim in ancient gorges and jump from cool waterfalls in the tropical heat. Camping under the stars and living with no schedule, all of this was incredible. But for all of God's glory and beauty He shared, it was one glance at my children that taught me what child-like trust looked like.

I returned from that trip with a new understanding. Things happen to people all the time: good, bad, big and small. It is the nature of life. It is inevitable. As the bumper sticker says, 'Stuff happens!' One thing through all of this is certain, if the Lord is my shepherd, then He is out in front and leads me through it all. There is nothing else I need. Surely goodness and mercy will follow me all the days of my life.

My struggle with anxiety sometimes rears up and tries to claim my peace, but I am learning to turn my head back towards my driver. He knows the roads, He knows the ruts, and He alone knows how to steer through it all.

A Ghost of an Idea

Rory O'Donnell

When you're confronted with freedom, choices tend to rush at you with overwhelming fervour.

As I sit in my office, mindlessly scrolling through my graduation photos from three years ago, I hear muffled and unbidden sounds from my electric piano downstairs.

No one should be home yet, I realise. My hands grow clammy. *Of course, there's an intruder the one time I'm alone.* I step with silent feet to the stairwell, the question of what they could want, and why they were showcasing their music skills flicking into my mind.

I take the steps one at a time, the notes developing into song…until my foot cracks, and the harmonies come to a deafening stop. I don't stand there for long. A flash of blue flees from the piano to my room, and with a pulsing heart, I follow.

There, floating above my guitar in the tight space between my loaded bookshelf and dresser, was a ghost. I would be shocked at his presence, but my curiosity was stronger.

'What are you doing here?' I ask.

He merely sniggers in response. He nods to the guitar. 'You gonna play?'

It sounds appealing, but before I can ask for clarification, he flies straight for me, into my mind.

I like playing the guitar…and the piano…and the drums, only I don't have a drum-kit. When I bought my guitar, the thought of recording music seemed so cool. I've thought about getting a cord and recording software to actually do it, but I haven't yet. The idea keeps flying through my head though. What's stopping me from recording music, other than money? I've been working on an acoustic version of my friend's song from school. Come to think of it, I should work out the piano part for that. Also, my sister really wants me to arrange the music for a Broadway adaptation of—

My phone's ringtone disrupts my musing, the rhythmic vibrations from my pocket urging me to answer. The number belongs to my university classmate, Kedy. 'Hello?' I answer.

'Rory,' she begins in a whisper, 'you're alright!'

'Why wouldn't I be?'

She hesitates. I hear someone hum in the background. I ask, 'Are *you* alright?'

'There's some blue guy here who looks like you – has your eyes…but he's glowing and a bit transparent. He's not letting me leave…'

Another ghost! 'Where are you, Kedy?' I hope she hears the urgency in my voice.

'In our classroom at the uni.'

I tell her I'm on my way and I hustle out the door, my wallet, keys, and phone in tow as I race to the car.

'How do you foreshadow an overwhelming situation?'

I flinch. A blue ghost with a pen and paper, feet on my car's dashboard, stares at me from the passenger seat. His question hangs in the stale air.

'How'd *you* get in here?' I chuckle. The ghost's face, comically pinched in thought, requires significant effort to not laugh at.

A Ghost of an Idea

He claps his hands with an excited yelp. 'I've got it!' He buries his face in his paper, any sinister motives at least disguised. I start the drive through a growing fog, characteristic of the town.

My backlog of story ideas is growing. One of them is for a competition this year; another is a spin-off of a series-of-sorts that I wrote last year. I suppose that's part of the writer's life: you have ideas, and you can't shake them until you put them into words. Everything is inspiration, and ideas assault me randomly, like when plot points for a memoir distract me during a psychology lecture, or when I'm at church reading the iconic Old Testament stories.

In my spin-off project, one of the characters writes a song about being in a simulation, meaning I need to write a song about being in a simulation. Though why should I stop at simply lyrics?

The musician ghost speaks, 'You could totally make this song and put it on Spotify.'

I assent.

The writer ghost pipes in, 'And what if you made the migration story about the armour of God?'

A wave of motivation washes over me as he flies into my mind, though I have to stifle it as I park my car. The university campus is in its usual ghost-town state, though the fog makes it even more ominous. The trees are darkened with moisture, silhouettes fading into view as I walk the brick path to the classroom. I find the fog mysterious, but the question of where these ghosts are coming from looms over me with a greater shadow.

'Write a story about this,' the writer ghost murmurs.

'Make it a musical,' the musician ghost mutters.

I like both ideas; I'll try when I get home.

The classroom door creaks as it opens, removing any element of surprise. Kedy turns her head, and so does the ghost. She appears relieved at my arrival. The ghost's expression, however, is difficult to read, though it seems as though he's listening very intently, planning on remembering every word that leaves my mouth.

I chose to study psychology because its prospects were good, and I had an interest in it, not to mention the lack of other options. Toowoomba didn't have any physiotherapy degrees, and I wasn't interested in aviation – both suggestions from my parents. I'd love to understand how brains work and how to help people through that, but something within me is dissatisfied. I wonder if I *should* switch to physiotherapy like mom says…but I'd feel as if I was giving up on psychology. Maybe counselling would be a pathway more suited for me? There's a Christian seminary overseas that offers a master's degree, but I'd need to complete my current degree first. I guess I should stay…

The psychologist ghost smirks and enters my mind.

Kedy says, 'What was that about?'

I change the subject. 'Are you fine?'

She nods. 'He said he was the last one.'

Interesting.

We say our good-byes, and I drive back home.

That night I lie in my bed. A single thought haunts me: it seemed the ghosts *wanted* to be caught.

'*Start the story.*'

'*Did you do enough study today?*'

'*Just play your guitar!*'

A Ghost of an Idea

Their boneless swirling unsettles me, voices haunting, cackles tormenting.

'*Should you do post-graduate study?*'

Probably.

'*Where will your stories take you?*'

Dunno. Somewhere, hopefully.

'*How will you use your musicianship?*'

At a church?

'Write. Play. Study,' they chant, with blue eyes like mine widened in a craze. I wouldn't mind it if they stopped. '*Choose one. Choose one. Choose one.*' Actually, I would most certainly like it if they stopped. '*One. One. One—*'

'GOD!' I cry out in the dark, and the ghosts freeze. 'I have these choices, but what am I meant to do?'

The ghosts vanish, and what began as a nudge in my stomach dissolves through my body, leaving a warm, lingering thought, '*You are who I made you to be, ideas and all. They will be useful. No need to rush.*'

I take a breath, these words a relaxant to my mind. I still have my life ahead of me. My studies could change, but I'll work hard where I'm at. I have an upcoming writer's retreat; I'll focus on my stories then. My guitar is always available; I'll keep practising a little when I'm able.

I meet up with the ghosts occasionally. Though they once were pushy, I'm glad I met them. I know how to deal with them now.

A Journey through the Shadows

Sandy S Lish

Karen waved from her porch, shouting, 'Where've you been the last two weeks?'

'North Carolina,' I hollered back to my new neighbour, whose larger-than-life folksiness shone through her petite stature.

'North Carolina? What were you doing there?' she asked. 'I thought you moved in from Virginia.' Karen's voice softened as she approached the edge of my sloped driveway.

'Oh, I did,' I chuckled. 'Wait until you hear what happened in North Carolina – and the rest of our wild summer story.'

Karen's eyes widened. 'I'm listening, girl,' she said, leaning closer.

At first, I hesitated. Privacy was my shield until Karen's unflinching gaze pierced through it.

I braced myself and slowly unravelled a story that began 92 days earlier in Virginia.

'It started on a mid-June afternoon when my Virginia Beach faculty gathered for one final meeting of the school year. In that quiet room, our principal thanked the staff for their accomplishments, then concluded by acknowledging those who would not be returning in the fall. I carefully listened as he called out each name. Then I heard mine. My heart raced as I nervously stood, pausing while my colleagues applauded. I smiled, but it masked my internal struggle. I wasn't psychologically prepared to say farewell.

'Several months earlier, my husband Andy, an electrical engineer, suggested relocating to a region with more high-tech companies. I initially agreed until he selected the Boston region as his top choice. That's when my fears set in, and the irrational "kicking and screaming" began.

'Over the next several weeks, I tried to persuade Andy to reconsider. "Let's not uproot the children from their stable environment." He listened.

'When that didn't gain enough traction, I raised other pressing concerns. "My parents live four hours away. What if they need us?" He listened more.

'After exhausting my options, I finally blurted out in desperation, "After sixteen years in the same school, classroom, and district, are you asking me to leave behind a career that has shaped my identity?"

'Like other times, Andy hugged me, brought me flowers, and offered hours of encouraging pep talks. But neither he nor I fully grasped the deeper issue – a scary, illogical giant lurking in my mind, taunting me with the fear of abandoning the security of my familiar, structured environment.

'My apprehensions soon confronted reality when I watched the realtor pound the "FOR SALE" sign onto our front lawn. I knew I needed to stop my resistance and embrace a different mindset. "I can't do this alone," I said to God. "I surrender to your guidance regardless of the outcome." From that prayer forward, a series of extraordinary events began to unfold, starting with my job hunt.

'I had been scouring the employment section of a Boston newspaper, hoping to find a teaching position within thirty miles of Nashua, New Hampshire – our soon-to-be home. After many unproductive searches, I stumbled upon a small posting for a part-time position in Billerica,

Massachusetts. I knew little about the state and nothing about Billerica or its proximity to Nashua. Still, I grabbed a pen, circled the classified ad, and set the newspaper aside for later research.

'The following day, I hosted a modest garage sale. Everything seemed normal as visitors stopped to rummage through kids' clothes and toys – until two women stepped out of a large van and into my driveway. The older woman inquired about the price of a hobbyhorse. Before I could respond, the younger woman reminded her mother that she couldn't transport it to her home.

'I raised my eyebrows as I glanced toward their van and thought, *What's the problem? They have plenty of space in that van!*

'"Let me explain," the woman's daughter said, noticing the puzzled look on my face. "My mother plans to return to Massachusetts in a few weeks."

'Excitedly remembering Nashua's proximity to Massachusetts, I said, "Massachusetts? I'm moving to Nashua, New Hampshire, this summer!"

'"My mother lives in Billerica, a Boston suburb about 20 miles from Nashua," she replied.

'"Billerica!" I remarked with surprise, remembering the obscure job posting I found in the newspaper the previous night. Our conversation immediately drifted to Billerica's school system and the surrounding community.

'A short while later, I watched the two women drive away in their white van, leaving me with a feeling that I couldn't shake. Had God heard my prayer and, in some unexpected way, steered them to my house to show me He was listening and guiding my direction?

A Journey through the Shadows

'As the summer wound down, my family and I said our goodbyes to friends, squeezed our two kids and a dog into our compact-sized car, and set off for a twelve-hour exodus to New Hampshire. After settling in, we were eager for a relaxing getaway to New York. But our respite abruptly ended when I received a long-distance call from my brother.

'Rather than his usual jovial hello, my brother's voice sounded frantic. "Something happened at Mom and Dad's place," he said, explaining that an arsonist had thrown a Molotov cocktail into the adjacent renter's window. Although our elderly parents were never the intended target, the fire and smoke damage left the entire duplex uninhabitable – and our parents homeless.

'Just like my brother, I was lost. He pleaded for support, but I snapped without thinking, "How can I help Mom and Dad in North Carolina tonight when we're hours away, even from our own home?" There was silence. I took a deep breath and softened my voice, promising, "I'll do my best to figure this out...even though I'm not sure how."

'Shortly after the phone call, despite our exhaustion, Andy and I decided to head back to New Hampshire. During that four-hour nighttime trip, limited conversations peppered the silence until we travelled through a dimly lit stretch of highway along Connecticut's Interstate 84. Then the mood changed.

'Our son shouted from the back seat, pointing out the car's window, "Look, Mom, that truck is from Roxboro!"

'"Roxboro!" I said with surprise.

'I initially thought he was mistaken – Roxboro, North Carolina, was my parents' small hometown, roughly 600 miles from our driving location in Connecticut.

'I turned, and to my astonishment, my son was correct. I, too, saw "Roxboro" printed on the leasing vehicle's cabin door.

'For the rest of our trip back home, we kept returning to the same question: "What are the chances of seeing a vehicle from Roxboro just hours after learning about the duplex fire?" Given my parents' predicament, it didn't feel like a coincidence. Instead, it felt like the wind against a boat's sail – nudging us forward. Perhaps God was reminding us that we were not alone in our struggles.

'Days after our move, with boxes still unpacked, I travelled to Roxboro alone to assess the situation. My arrival resembled a scene from a disaster film – my mom lay in a hospital, my dad was speaking gibberish from emotional shock, and their charred duplex still reeked of lingering smoke.

'Overwhelmed, I focused on finding them permanent housing. During my four-day trip, I toured several rental properties. Each failed visit left me more desperate. Out of options, I wrestled with an internal debate: keep searching or uproot my parents from their fifty years of life in Roxboro and move them to New Hampshire? I couldn't decide alone, so I called Andy.

'"It's going to be a big adjustment," he said, burdened by everything the summer had demanded of us. His initial hesitation worried me. I listened carefully as he brought up the Roxboro truck again. Then, calmly, he added, "The Lord is in control."'

'What a story, huh?' I said to Karen, laughing despite everything we endured.

Karen shook her head in disbelief. 'If I had read your adventure in a book, I would have thought it was fiction!'

'And your parents?' she asked. 'Where are they now?'

I pointed toward my house. 'They're here, but only temporarily. When both parents arrived under one roof, we quickly realised they couldn't climb the stairs to the bedrooms. For now, Mom sleeps on one couch and Dad on the other.'

Karen embraced me tightly. 'Let me know if I can help you,' she offered before returning to her house.

As I watched her walk away, I couldn't help but reflect on my family and the series of changes that we had experienced over the last 92 days – our children had enrolled in their new schools; I had joined the Billerica Memorial High School faculty; Andy was pursuing his consulting career in the Boston area; and my parents were emotionally struggling with the loss of their home. Despite these hurdles, we clung to God, believing that the One who had lovingly led us this far through uncertainty would continue guiding us through our journey.

Birthday Cake Faith

Natalie Ingram

Growing up, I always knew my parents loved me and my four older siblings very much. Dad worked hard to save money to not only provide for our basic needs, but also so that he could afford to take us on holidays around Australia. We never made it to the Northern Territory or to Western Australia as a family, but we got to every other state! Dad also endeavoured to give my siblings and me regular pocket money, movies and video games.

Mum always provided the family with food and quality first-aid, both of which she was excellent at. But, even more important to me at the time was her tradition of making a special cake of our choice from the *Women's Weekly Birthday Cake* book, until we turned ten. She'd create it for us the night before our birthday. I remember choosing the piano cake for my tenth birthday which, to this day, bemuses me greatly as I didn't enjoy piano lessons at all! Nevertheless, Mum made that cake for me, and one of my sisters created a little music book out of cardboard for it, titling it 'As Time Goes By'. My goodness, that cake looked amazing!

Like every family though, we had troubles. Ours stemmed from the fact we were part of a cult and we only left it the year I turned twenty-one.

Looking back, I realise my childhood was severely battered by that place. It controlled my schooling, my sport, my Sunday church services and my Bible studies. I was never allowed choices, never treated like I had an intelligent mind, and always expected to do what I was told by the powers that be, regardless of my feelings. Deliberate disobedience or an inability to perform to their often unclear standards resulted in humiliation and harsh consequences. I was declared 'lazy' if I struggled with homework and then told I was 'prideful' or 'deceitful' if I tried to explain why. I quickly learned that I was always going to be 'wrong' in their eyes and honesty was impossible. Most weeks I was brought to tears in front of my class and daily I went home feeling totally inadequate.

I'm very thankful that at least in my home-life, I was genuinely loved as a person because of who my parents were. When Dad saved up to buy us 'unnecessary' fun things, and when he budgeted for family holidays, when Mum looked after us every time we were hurt and provided our meals, when she insisted on giving each of us a special cake from that precious birthday book – my parents were doing so because they loved us and because their faith in God assured them that it was good.

To the End of their Days

Lynda Worrell

As a young teenager, I had a life-changing encounter with God at a youth camp in the Adelaide Hills. I came home glowing with joy, born again and excited to share my new faith. I told my dad everything – about Jesus, about a woman whose bulging varicose veins disappeared after prayer, about the presence of God I had felt so powerfully. But Dad didn't know what to do with me. He listened but didn't engage. Often, I was met with silence, or a quick impatient change of subject. His heart seemed closed to God, and I grieved over this.

In 2002, my dad was diagnosed with mesothelioma, a cancer caused by asbestos exposure. True to his private nature and fear of hospitals, he failed to tell our family for five long months. I was devastated – not just by the news of his illness, but by the fear I'd always carried: that he would leave this life without ever knowing Jesus. I cried out to God in those days, not knowing how to penetrate the wall he had built around his heart. My fear of losing him for eternity was more painful than the thought of losing him in this life. The night he told us, I could only let go and deliberately release him into God's care.

Within days, something unexpected happened. My father came to me privately and asked, 'Why haven't you offered to pray for me?' I was stunned. I had stopped offering because I had become discouraged, even hardened. I didn't want another rejection. That small question opened the door. At that moment, I had the honour of leading my dad to Jesus. He found peace – true, eternal peace.

To the End of their Days

When Dad passed away in March 2003, everything changed for Mum. They had been married for fifty-six years, and she had relied on him for everything – managing money, writing letters, dealing with household affairs. Dad had asked me to ensure Mum was cared for.

Simple tasks like banking, using debit cards or even catching a bus were overwhelming. Dad had always overseen those sorts of things. Later that year, I accompanied Mum to the UK to see her sisters and her family whom she hadn't seen in fifty years. That journey brought her joy and healing, a break in the weight of her grief.

About eighteen months after Dad died, Mum began to speak tentatively about companionship. Not another husband, necessarily – just someone to go op-shopping with, visit markets, and sit down for a chat over a cup of tea. I didn't know what to think. She was 76, dealing with health issues, and beginning to show signs of memory decline. But there was a spark of hope in her voice.

I remembered hearing about a minister telling his congregation about asking God specifically for what you want in relationships. So I encouraged Mum to pray – and she did. She even wrote a list. 'He has to be tall – he must have a good sense of humour and like going out.' It was touching and bold, and she truly believed God was listening. I wasn't so confident.

Meanwhile, God was stirring something in my husband John and me. Twenty years earlier, we had received a call to leave our home and take the gospel to everyday Australians – the kind of people who wouldn't be found sitting in a church pew. We had spent those early years visiting festivals, pubs, gem-fields, and rural and coastal towns, meeting people where they were and simply sharing Jesus.

Now, twenty years later, that same calling was reigniting. Stronger. Clearer. We felt the Lord saying again, 'Go to the everyday Aussie – he's still not sitting in the church.' This time, we sensed the direction was ten hours' drive west of the Sunshine Coast towards rural and remote Queensland, where drought and hardship were pressing down on communities.

But one big question weighed heavily on our hearts: *What about Mum?* She was in a one-room unit at an aged care facility – and she hated it. She'd rebel against the routines, refusing to sign the fire register and even hopping on the public bus without telling anyone. She wasn't happy with meals being chosen and prepared for her, and insisted on buying her own groceries, stuffing them into a tiny fridge meant only for milk and a few small items – so full that she couldn't close the door properly. She still had her spark, but she needed care. God assured us that He was going to meet every need we had.

In February 2005, our family offered to keep an eye on Mum while we took a five-week break from our jobs in Queensland Health, to test the waters. We headed west in faith, travelling from cattle station to cattle station, sharing with people who were still going through terrible drought and other challenges. The stories we heard were heartbreaking. The land was dry, and so were many of the hearts.

As the weeks passed, it became clear that this was more than a test run. God was calling us back to this mission – not just for a season, but for the next chapter of our lives. Just as we were preparing to return home and pondering about how we could do this, something else was unfolding back home that we hadn't expected.

Mum called us to say that she received a phone call from a man named Jack. He had come across an ad for a companion for outings, in the *Queensland Seniors* newspaper – months after we submitted it. We had forgotten about that ad.

To the End of their Days

They arranged to meet at a café near Mum's place. Jack turned out to be warm, respectful, and funny. He had recently moved to the area and was looking for a companion for outings, just like my mum was.

I don't think I could have accepted another man in my mother's life – unless God Himself prepared me for it. And that's exactly what He did. At this time, I had a dream that I will never forget. It was vivid – so clear, it felt almost tangible.

In the dream, I saw my father appear at the front door of our family home. He was dressed in a formal suit. Inside the house, a large family gathering was underway, and I knew instinctively that it was the afternoon. My first thought was that Dad was heading to a funeral. My heart sank – was this a warning that Mum was going to pass away? After all, Mum was the one with long term health issues.

But then I noticed something: Dad looked radiant. Healthy. Free. As if a great burden had been lifted from him. It struck me then – *God had changed my father so much in such a brief time since he passed away, while I had spent a lifetime sensing and trying to ease his burdens.*

Then he spoke to me, though not with audible words. I clearly heard him say, 'You will no longer be fully responsible for your mother.'

For a moment, my heart fell, and I thought, 'Didn't I do a good enough job?' Then a beautiful wave of the love of a father and husband issued forth from him. I knew the source was God. It wasn't correction – it was release. A blessing. Permission to let go of a commitment which I had been holding onto so tightly.

That dream, more than anything, prepared my heart. It gave me peace to accept what was about to unfold. It softened my spirit to embrace Jack – not as a replacement for my father, but as a God-given answer to my mother's quiet, faithful prayers.

A few months later, Jack asked my husband and I if he could have my mum's hand in marriage. He wanted us to know he was serious. He genuinely cared for her and wanted to honour her. It was such a tender moment. We saw in Jack the integrity, loyalty, and warmth.

My husband responded to Jack's request with, 'There are just two provisions – no returns and no babies!' They were married in September 2005.

Mum and Jack spent three beautiful years together. They enjoyed laughter, many adventures, and companionship. Jack became part of our family. By the way, Jack was very tall, with huge feet and a big sense of humour. We now had freedom to follow our calling, knowing that Mum was loved and safe. She could leave the aged-care centre also!

Looking back, I see how God wove all of this together. A father's salvation. A mother's prayer. A newspaper ad answered in perfect time. A dream that brought peace. It reminds me that God never forgets the cries of our hearts – and He delights in writing stories we could never imagine.

I thank God for His sense of humour: my mum's surname before she married my father was Coffee, her mother's name was Ham, her aunt's name was Lamb, and now she was married to Jack Spicer.

A Whisper Away

June Hopkins

There it was again – the sound of voices outside my bedroom window. I had lain awake, silent and still for a couple of minutes, listening. Two male voices spoke in low tones directly below my window. My heart began to race as I considered my options. It was 2:30am so I knew that they were probably intent on a break and enter, perhaps to gain the keys to my car, housed in the closed garage. The car is sixteen years old, so I thought it highly unlikely they'd want it once they saw it. The news had recently carried too many stories of young people breaking into homes in the early hours, even while families were asleep in the house. They mostly stole cars for joyrides; however, some teenagers became violent if threatened.

I live alone and am disabled so I knew I would be no match if they should manage to enter. I whispered an urgent prayer, asking God for divine protection and wisdom in the circumstances. Bible verses that I'd learned as a young person came immediately to mind. Psalm 91:5 'Do not be afraid of the terror by night', and Deuteronomy 31:6 'Be strong and of good courage, fear not, nor be afraid of them.' The verses calmed me. The intruders sounded like they were moving towards the back of my house.

Due to a personal situation when I'd purchased my home, the sellers had been present during my preliminary inspection. The husband told me they were Christians and had prayed for the house to sell to the person of God's choosing. I told them I was also a Christian. I liked what I saw, and we believed I was the right person to purchase their well-loved home. The wife told me that ladies from her church had helped wash all the walls and had prayed for protection of the potential buyer as they cleaned. It made me feel safe as I moved in. Remembering that conversation brought me a steadily growing peace as I heard the footsteps traverse my back yard this night.

Thankfully, at my family's insistence, I had recently installed prowler-proof, triple-locked screen doors on all four entry points, plus I had grills on my windows.

After a couple more minutes, I heard the click of the side gate. The intruders were moving away from my place. I peeked through a window and saw a police car drive along the street with lights flashing. A second car came a minute later. I was able to see two constables running on foot searching for the culprits. They must have been called when other places were targeted before mine. Shortly after, they returned with a teenage boy, arms handcuffed behind him. Within minutes, there were three young people sitting on the gutter edge surrounded by police.

I believe that God was with me during this experience, reminding me that He is only a whisper away from each one of us.

Chosen

Carolyn Tonkin

I saw her walking towards me.

Same brown hair. Same purposeful stride – she even swung her hips like Mum.

I increased my pace, trying not to run but leaving my husband and daughters in my wake, as raw emotion bubbled up and threatened to spill over, because the moment had finally arrived.

We came face to face as the sunshine peeped through the gum trees in the caravan park where they were staying, and an image of my grandfather's gorgeous blue eyes flashed across my consciousness.

'Hello,' I said.

I couldn't help but stare. This was my sister, my own flesh and blood. The moment seemed surreal, but I opened my arms to her and invited her into my world.

She didn't hesitate. She threw herself against my chest and the floodgates opened; years of wondering where she was, what she looked like, and how her voice sounded, now overflowing into choked sobs of instant connection.

When we finally broke our hold, both families had caught up with us and were standing together, grinning awkwardly at one another.

I wiped my eyes. She blew her nose. And we laughed at their embarrassment.

'Sorry, Kris, where's my manners? This is my husband, Rob, and two of our daughters, Andrea and Hannah.'

Rob went in for a hug. 'It's good to meet you,' he said, his voice uncharacteristically shaky. He extended his hand to Kris's husband. 'G'day.'

'Sorry, this is Barry,' Kris said.

He took Rob's hand in a strong grip. 'This has been a long time coming, hasn't it?'

'It has,' I interrupted, 'but it doesn't matter, we're here now and I am stoked to meet you. All of you.'

Kris turned to her two teenage children. 'Claire. Jonothan. Meet your auntie.'

'Hello,' they said in unison, shifting their feet and glancing at one another.

Poor things. Thrust into a situation not of their own choosing. In fact, none of us chose it. Our parents did.

I looked around for a place to go – the men had already begun chatting and the kids drifted towards one another. 'Let's sit in the barbeque area, it's shaded.'

We made our way to a covered picnic table and swung our legs over the seats. Our daughters sat opposite, already comfortable in each other's presence.

'I see you've also inherited our father's Irish skin.' I held out my arms. 'Freckles. Gotta love 'em. I never tan in the sun, I just burn and gather a few more – sun-kisses my Nanna called them.' I glanced at my sister. 'Our Nanna. Sorry.'

'It's okay,' she laughed. 'I had a Gran too.'

'Of course you did,' I laughed.

Chosen

Kris's daughter, Claire, giggled and whispered something to Andrea and Hannah. All three looked at us and grinned.

'What?' Kris said.

'You laugh the same,' Claire said.

'And you have the same hook nose as Mum and me,' Hannah added.

Kris and I turned to each other and smiled.

'Well, it's not surprising, we're sisters, made from the same recipe, and clearly the genes are strong. But I still don't know where my green eyes come from. No-one else in the family has green eyes, they all have blue eyes, like yours, Kris.'

'You must be a throwback from somewhere down the line,' she chuckled.

'Yeah, probably on my dad's…' I sighed, 'Sorry, I mean our dad's side.' I looked at her with eyes that a puppy dog would be proud of.

Kris rested her hand on my forearm and held my gaze. 'It's okay. We'll both need to adjust.'

I struggled to not burst into tears again, as another wave of emotion hit me. I cleared my throat and nodded.

How could she be so relaxed? So full of grace? I had known that she existed for decades. I still remember the day Mum sat my brother and I down at the kitchen table with the introduction, 'I have something to tell you.'

What a secret to keep.

All these years later, coming face-to-face with my sister, I still struggled to understand how any mother could give one child away, while keeping the others. It could have been me. But it wasn't, and I felt guilty, and sad, and angry, all at the same time. Guilty that it was her, not me. Sad that we didn't grow up together like normal sisters, and angry that my parents couldn't work out their differences so we could be a family.

'When did you first know you were adopted?' I asked her.

'I can't remember how old I was, but I must have been young because I feel like I've always known. My parents told me I was chosen. My brother was the same. We are both adopted.'

'Chosen,' I nodded. 'I like that.' It reminded me of something a minister had said in a sermon at church. He'd said, God chooses us; we don't choose him. I remembered because I thought I had chosen God, not the other way around. He chose me to be his child, just like her parents chose her.

'So you weren't sad about it? Did you ever wonder who your parents were?' I asked.

She thought for a moment. 'No, not really. I was happy where I was, and I knew I was loved. I didn't think I'd missed out on anything.'

'So why did you say yes, when you received the letter to say my parents wanted to meet you?'

She nodded. 'I didn't at first. But as the months went on, I became curious and once I knew I had other siblings, the questions began. What were they like? Did they know about me? Why was I musical but the rest of my family wasn't?'

'You're musical? Oh, we've got so much to talk about!'

'You too?' she asked.

I nodded. 'But I get it. Ever since I was a teenager, I would look at girls a few years younger than me walking along the street and wonder if they were you.' I chuckled. 'Crazy, I know.'

Chosen

She put her arm around my shoulder. 'Well, we don't have to wonder any longer. We can ask each other all the questions we want.'

An impish smile crept across my face, and I turned my body towards her. 'Okay, first question. How many boyfriends did you have before Barry?'

We both laughed. I glanced over to my daughters whose mouths hung open. 'What? Too personal? Okay, okay.' I laughed again as I reset my backside on the hard wooden seat. 'How about this? What are your mum and dad like?'

She nodded.

'My dad died when I was three, so I don't really remember him, but my Mum is great. She's fun and full of life.'

'How did she feel about you meeting your biological family?'

'She understood. She knew this day might come, but it doesn't change how I feel about her – she's still my mum. She told me it was my choice.'

'I love that. I hope I get to meet her one day.'

'What was your upbringing like?' she asked.

'It was…interesting. I grew up with my grandparents. They were great, they created a stable environment for us, but Mum struggled with her emotions. Dad wasn't around; I only met him properly a few years ago…but that's a story for another time.'

A playful grin covered my sister's face. 'So…how many boyfriends did you have?'

'Ha! Touché. A few but nothing too serious until Rob came along. It was hard growing up without a dad, and Mum didn't encourage boyfriends. I think she felt all men were untrustworthy after Dad left us – not that I remember, I was barely three.'

'Interesting that we both grew up without our dads,' she said.

'Yeah, something else we have in common. But one thing my grandparents taught me was that although my earthly father wasn't around, I had a father in heaven.'

Kris frowned. 'You mean God?'

'Yes. I can't see him or touch him on earth, but I can feel him. And just like your mum told you that you were chosen, I believe God chose us to be sisters. He saw us in our mother's womb before we even entered the world. He knew the families we would grow up in, and he also knew that one day we would meet.'

'Okay...' she said.

I knew I'd said too much. I'd overwhelmed her. I'd assumed things. I'd forgotten that she didn't have the same experiences as me.

'Anyway, that's just me,' I said.

She nodded and I looked over to our three girls who were sitting quietly. 'Do you want to ask the dads if they're ready for lunch?'

The three of them took off to find their fathers.

I turned to her. 'I'm sorry if I came on too strong.'

She looked at me with gentle eyes. 'It's okay. We have so much to process and this is just the beginning.'

Redhead

Roslyn Bradshaw

'I don't want a red-haired sister!' My six-year-old sister complained at my birth.

And when I discovered that red hair was not common, I wasn't sure if I wanted to be a redhead. I preferred not to stand out in a crowd. However, the world was a fascinating place, and when I wasn't busy exploring or soaking up knowledge, I read stories. I could be transported away by immersing myself in the adventures of the *Famous Five* or the *Secret Seven*. The *Silver Brumby* series of novels fuelled an obsession with horses, and I dreamed of riding through the high country of the Snowy Mountains. The colour of my hair didn't matter.

Every morning before school, Mum patiently twisted my thick hair into two long plaits. Even on Saturdays and Sundays, my luxurious locks were restrained in braids. One day, as I walked home from school, a boy behind me called out, 'Hey, Carrots!' Then four boys ran past, yelling, 'Redhead! Redhead!' I was bewildered, unsure how to react, so I kept walking. At home, my father told me to retort, 'Sticks and stones may break my bones, but names will never hurt me.' Dad had been called Four Eyes for wearing glasses and Swot for being studious, but I didn't want to provoke any fights, so I ignored the teasing.

Appearances weren't made much of in our home, and I didn't go to a hairdresser until Grade Seven. I don't remember why my long plaits were severed and my hair styled into a short bob. I do remember going home, looking at myself in the mirror, and bursting into tears. Without my long, red hair, I felt like I had lost part of my identity. Regular trips to the salon kept my hair neat and short, albeit long enough to secure in a bun for ballet performances. With a busy life of netball, horse-riding, ballet, piano lessons and tennis, I didn't have time to fuss with my hair. The only time I really thought about my hair colour was when I read in *Dolly Magazine* that redheads often appear unattractive when their hair turns grey, and I didn't want to think about that.

Nicknames are interesting. The boys had given up taunting me with 'Carrots', but at the stables where I rode daily Mr. Robertson called me 'Blue'. The first time I heard it I was surprised, not realising that it was a way of referring to my red hair. However, when Mr. Robertson called me 'Blue', it wasn't in a teasing tone, but more a friendly way of acknowledging my auburn-coloured hair – an Aussie thing.

As a teenager, I became more self-conscious. After we moved to Wudinna during Year 10, I kept my hair at a medium length to avoid the tangles. Sometimes, for a dance or special occasion, I used rollers to curl the bottom of my hair, enduring the prickly plastic rollers all night. The curls never stayed in for long, to my dismay. Fashion magazines advised redheads not to wear red or pink, but rather yellow, green and autumn tones, so I selected fabrics for the clothes I sewed accordingly.

During Years 11 and 12, at Port Lincoln High School, life became even more full, with study, leadership responsibilities, team sports and athletics. I learned that standing out in a crowd came with the territory of wanting to excel. I even had to make speeches in my role of House Captain.

Recently, a friend from high school recalled, 'I can still see you sprinting down the track in your Eyre House uniform. You ran like the wind.'

I smiled. 'I'm not doing much running now.'

'But you still look athletic,' he appraised. 'You won some academic awards too, didn't you?'

My heart beat faster. My eyes darted around the crowd. *How to reply without sounding boastful?* I nervously admitted, 'Yes, I won all sorts of awards.'

Why was I still embarrassed to admit to my achievements? Tall Poppy Syndrome? How could I be pleased and self-conscious at the same time? Not wanting to stand out, but not willing to be anything less than my best self. Perhaps the only way I could escape my insecurities was to forget about other people, aiming to give my personal best, whatever I was involved in.

During my Rotary Exchange gap year, my Japanese schoolmates were envious of both my hair colour and its waves, yet their straight ebony hair suited them. There, I really stood out. I was taller than them all, and there was great hilarity when the yearly health check revealed that I was a metre around the hips! I was taken aback, but pragmatism quickly took over. If I were taller, of course I would be wider as well, so I just laughed along with them.

Back in Adelaide, immersed in university study and extra-curricular activities, I enjoyed a time of explosive growth mentally, socially and spiritually. The Jesus Revolution was breathing new life into churches all over Adelaide, and Christians on campus were no exception. We had cell groups, pop concerts, communal meals, Bible Studies and public debates on controversial topics. Charismatic groups encouraged the use of spiritual gifts.

One day in a prayer meeting, someone had a prophetic word for me. 'God, your heavenly Father, loves you so much.'

My gut reaction startled me. I didn't realise I felt unworthy of God's love. I heard Jesus whisper, 'I have made you worthy.' I struggled to accept that it could be true, but as I received God's affirmation, something happened in me. Tears flowing, I sobbed convulsively until my burden lifted. When I walked out of that upstairs room, I had a new sense of self-worth. I was loved.

Then came marriage, family and my lifelong vocation as a missionary Bible College lecturer. Again, busy fulfilling times. As I aged, I started pulling out the silver hairs, as one does. In Kiev, a pastor's wife said, 'Why don't you go to the beauty salon? It's not expensive, and everybody does it.' So I spent time matching my original hair colour and went regularly to the same hairdresser. Back in Australia, even though it became increasingly expensive, I kept dyeing my hair red until pressure from my children mounted.

'Vanity, vanity, all is vanity,' said one.

Another suggested, 'Grey hair is the glory of the aged and a sign of maturity. Let people see that you have weathered the years and have wisdom worth mining.'

'That *is* biblical,' I admitted wryly.

Yet I wrestled with self-doubt. Our society adulates youth. I didn't want to be thought of as old. I was afraid of the stereotypes. But should I pretend to be younger than I was? I was conflicted. How often had I told others that God was pleased with each unique person He had created? What was happening to me?

I thought, *If I knew that my hair was all white, I could do it*. The idea planted in my youth that redheads went grey in an ugly way resurfaced. But there were wider issues. I *was* ageing. My eyesight wasn't as good as it used to be, and neither was my memory. I *was* having to slow down. I needed to embrace this season of life with grace and enjoy the person God had created me to be. *Your hair colour isn't that important,* I told myself. Yet everywhere I went, I saw people dyeing their hair. I was afraid to change.

'Mum, there are different ways to transition to grey if you want to. Do some research on the internet.'

My daughter was right. After much agonising, I stopped dyeing my hair. Three months later, as the colour grew out, I had a cap dye, with narrow streaks of a blonde-gold colour. My hairdresser graded my hair to encourage its natural curl, and I felt positive about my look. My friends said it looked good.

Six months later, I had the cap treatment again, to disguise the last of the colour line. I did have some natural colour left, but it was lighter. The waves were easy to manage. The transition was less stressful than I had anticipated. Some women began emulating me, moving away from covering the grey. Not only that, embracing grey hair was trending with film stars!

Now I know that how God made me is still good. I don't need to wonder if I would be better off different. One neighbour says he prefers my hair how it was, but his wife says she likes it now. Everyone is entitled to their own opinion, but I want to focus on what is important to me.

'You are wonderfully created. I have made you worthy. I love you so much.'

Thank you, Lord, for reminding me. I lost the plot somehow along the way.

Each age and stage *is* manageable, perhaps with some help from the hairdresser.

No more fear.

God's Light in the Darkness

Hazel Barker

Every Sunday, we gathered around the dining table for a cherished ritual – chicken curry with rice, manna from heaven. The spices, so delicately balanced, were not just a culinary delight but a reminder of the blessings bestowed upon us.

On this Sunday, as the tantalising aroma filled the air, we sat wide-eyed and full of expectation. The cook entered, carrying a steaming dish – a physical manifestation of sustenance and provision. Mum began to serve with trembling hands, giving the drumsticks to Rupert and Bertie, while Dad received two chicken thighs.

The tranquillity shattered. Dad's voice thundered in anger, demanding the drumstick. He grabbed the dish and flung it into the air. The bowl became a comet of fury, hurtling across the room and crashing to the ground.

The cook fell to his knees, cleaning the floor with care. He swept away the broken fragments, leaving only the aroma of spices and a reminder of how God holds us when life feels fragmented.

I sat frozen at the table, my heart racing with fear and anguish for Mum. Her sacrifices, her trembling hands, her tears were all acts of love that reflected her nurturing spirit. Though the oppressive silence weighed heavily, I prayed, seeking God's guidance for the storm raging within our family.

In that moment of chaos, I felt the presence of God – a silent comfort amid fear.

God's Light in the Darkness

Dad stormed out of the room, consumed by his anger, leaving us shaken but alive. Rupert, usually outspoken, remained silent – a silence like a prayer. Mum retreated with tears streaming down her face, her faith carrying her even when her strength faltered.

But God did not forsake us. He delivered us from the tyranny overshadowing our lives. His love and protection paved a path for freedom and healing. Dad's wrathful presence no longer held sway over us. We rebuilt our lives with faith as our cornerstone. Mum's strength, rooted in God's love, became a beacon, guiding us out of the darkness.

Ten years later, when my father attempted to molest me, Mum found the strength to leave. She fled with us and took refuge in a convent – a sanctuary of peace after years of turmoil.

God's light has carried us forward, illuminating the path from despair to redemption. Our family now stands united, forever grateful for the deliverance we received. With hearts full of love and gratitude, we celebrate our blessings.

Now, as I reflect on those turbulent times, I realise how God's hand was present in every moment – strengthening Mum, shielding us children, and ultimately breaking the chains that bound us. His grace turned our sorrow into hope and fear into faith, proving that even in the darkest valleys, His light never ceases to shine.

Saying Goodbye to Faith
Elizabeth D Guntrip

Faith and I became friends in the 70's when our toddlers started preschool together. I thought of her as a hippie with alternative ideas about nutrition. We had wonderful long chats, often deep, always interesting. We routinely stood outside the kindy, chatting, after seeing our littlies inside and before going home to our chores.

Life went on, we left that country town and went our separate ways, but we had this in common – both her son and my daughter died comparatively young in somewhat broken circumstances. It was a shared grief. As we aged, although we lived some distance apart, we made the effort to drive to a halfway point at least once a year for a catch up over a leisurely lunch. It was pure pleasure. Faith had a big laugh and these were plentiful. She would throw her head back, giving voice to her enjoyment but never sounding raucous. I, on the other hand, had to temper my mirth, lest fellow diners look around in concern and wonder who let the riff raff in!

Faith's battle with illness is a story of triumph. She lost weight and her hair to a virulent cancer, but in the end, against the odds, she came back to life in what the medical fraternity calls 'remission', with her giving all thanks and praise to God for the miraculous result. Her *joie de vivre* was contagious. She took up her passion for cooking once more. Morning tea with her was never so simple as Vegemite toast. At her house you would be served such delicacies as mini key lime tarts, homemade cheddar biscuits and finger sandwiches garnished with watercress which might be called a fancy name like rainbow ribbon stacks, alongside watermelon refresher. And her dinners…well, they were gourmet works of art.

Saying Goodbye to Faith

We had Faith for at least ten more years. What a blessing. When she sent me a message to say she was in a hospice, I was horrified. Post-haste, I reorganised my diary, rearranging my schedule so that I could visit. The round trip would take up most of the day so I wanted our time together to be meaningful. I prayed about what I would say. What *do* you say?! For her part, Faith explained that although during the first episode with cancer she had fought determinedly, full of faith, this time she was greatly at peace with going to meet the Lord.

'I'm ready,' she said.

One of her nieces responded, 'You may be ready to go, Auntie Faith, but I'm not ready to let you go!'

My husband and I made the trip north, arriving late morning. He carried the basket I had prepared into the private room where Faith lay, a shadow of her exuberant former self. It was all I could do not to burst into tears at the sight of her, so frail and wracked, bravely smiling at us. How difficult it was to find the balance between over-cheerful and maudlin, but still genuine.

Our greeting was as warm as ever. Then I broached the agenda I had, by asking Faith if she would like me to serve her communion. She was thrilled. I set out my little travel communion set on her mobile tray, then said, 'First, would you allow me to wash your feet and refresh you in body and spirit?'

She laughed at that idea as she said, 'Yes.'

I folded back the sheet covering Faith's painfully thin feet and lifted them onto a towel, while my husband filled the small plastic bowl I had brought with tepid water. After the token washing, I anointed her feet with fragrant rose geranium oil, mixed with my tears, then did the same to her slim hands. I cherish the memory of her look of contentment as I massaged her bony fingers.

I had brought along a rather beautiful bone china cup and saucer that had been gifted to me. I poured in some pure spring water and served it to Faith, with words to the effect that she was a woman of the Most High God and I was giving her a cup of cold water in His name. Her eyes smiled at me over the rim as she sipped. I left the cup with her.

Communion was just as beautiful. Another visitor arrived and joined us in celebrating all that Christ did to make eternal life a reality for his followers, a prospect very close for Faith. I finished with a brief devotional word. Our whole visit took only thirty minutes, but its impact accounted for a great deal more of something vital yet intangible. Faith went into a coma soon after and died before the week was out. How glad I was that I did not delay in going to visit her by even a day. Her husband told me how joyfully she had spoken about that visit and told all her visitors about it.

Farewell, dear friend. See you in heaven.

Fragile

Kezia Pettitt

She's fragile.

You wouldn't know it, looking at her. Mid-thirties, she's just a tad taller than other women. Her brown hair, streaked with gold under the sunlight, tumbles in loose curls from her ponytail at the nape of her neck. Always in jeans and sneakers, as though ready to run at any moment. Sometimes she wonders about running away. This life she's created, with a menagerie of pets, a sprawling garden on the outskirts of the city, three children born from her own body.

Ah, yes. The children. Once, she'd had hazy dreams about these products of procreation. Most likely girls, as she came from a family of mostly daughters, as did her mother before her. There'd be endless seated craft activities, meandering walks alongside mossy creek beds, learning to braid daughters' hair. Baking and running and horse-riding, all the quintessentially girly things she'd longed to do with her own parents as a child.

Her first child? A boy. And not just any boy. This child, born loud, moved with the fury of a thunderstorm, whirling and lashing all about him. Sleepless little soul, he wailed long into the early pre-dawn hours, despite all the rocking and hushing. A being that craved movement, action, connection, at all hours.

Six weeks after she'd stopped breastfeeding him, she was pregnant again.

Another boy.

This one, a little quieter, although nocturnal. He'd sleep in five-hour stretches, cry for cuddles, cluster-feed for hours, his chubby little fist clutching at the fabric of his mother's shirt.

When he turned one, finally aware of the competition of his elder sibling, he'd discovered his voice. The volume from the two offspring doubled, each squabbling to be heard and held above the other.

Three. That's how old the firstborn was, when the diagnosis came. *Autism*. Exhausted, she learned to pour from a drained cup, her soul forever running on empty. Who else but her would navigate the systems, the schools, the side-eye glances?

Seven. The second was diagnosed at seven years old. School, once a joy for him, had lost its lustre. Withdrawn from the classroom, he no longer had to pretend to be like everyone else. Happy once more, as he swung himself upside-down on the couch, chatted about his preferred topic to sometimes unwilling audiences, spun things in endless circles.

The third? Another boy. Another one diagnosed at three years old.

Look at her. No – actually *look at her*. She seems powerful, doesn't she? Juggling the myriad needs of her three sons with seeming ease. Clashing calendars and schedules managed with grace, fluctuating capacity and a mishmash of needs carried carefully. Her little ones, growing, now not-so-little, thrive.

You wouldn't know it. She's fragile. About to break. At the end of her tether. Somehow, making it through, carried only by prayer and unseen grace. Be gentle with her, speak kindly to her, comfort her.

She's fragile.

Nan, What Took You So Long?

Raewyn Elsegood

'Nan back Friday?'

Jackson's two-year-old voice echoed in my mind as I finally walked through his front door, 24 hours later than promised. His chubby fingers had traced my face last Sunday as I'd whispered, 'Nan back Friday.' Those three simple words had become my mantra through what turned into the most unexpected journey home.

It started at Asheville airport, where a simple two-hour flight transformed into a comedy of biblical proportions. Three deplanings. Two different aircraft. Six hours of false starts. The airline staff looked as bewildered as we passengers felt, their apologetic smiles wearing thinner with each announcement of 'just a slight delay'. When they finally herded us outside like lost sheep, promising a shuttle to a hotel, I couldn't help but laugh. Here I was, a grandmother who'd just spent a beautiful week at the Blue Ridge Christian Writers Conference, now starring in my version of Groundhog Day.

The shuttle never came. The hotel had no rooms. The police officers who eventually rescued our stranded group delivered us to a hotel surrounded by fire trucks and emergency vehicles. 'Well,' I told my fellow travellers, 'at least we're consistent with the chaos.'

Four hours of sleep later, we were back at the airport for round two.

But somewhere between the third deplaning and the moment I finally collapsed into my seat, something shifted. Instead of fixating on Jackson's disappointed face, I noticed the surrounding faces. There were Jayce, Jill, Helen and Andrew from the writers' conference, clutching a week's worth of friendship and writing memories. Not wanting to let go, we had exchanged contact information and promised to encourage each other's writing journeys.

Then came the deplaned passengers, the business executive in the expensive suit, pacing and shouting into his phone about missing meetings. Parents attempting to distract their baby with food and songs. A couple trying to get to an engagement and a wedding the next day. The daughter who had just been to her mum's memorial. I listened until there was nothing left but to sit in silence together, strangers sharing the weight of time and missed appointments.

The overwhelmed airline agent managed a frustrated group of passengers. A social worker and myself helped him coordinate hotel arrangements, our years in the field proving useful in an airport crisis. His grateful smile reminded me why I'd become a chaplain.

But it was the two flight attendants on our third attempt who touched my heart most deeply. Sarah, the senior attendant, collapsed into the seat beside me during a fuelling attempt. One year ago to the day, her divorce had been finalised. She'd thought flying would distract her from the anniversary, but found herself trapped with her grief at thirty thousand feet. I held her hand as she cried, offering tissues and the kind of wordless comfort that only comes from having weathered your own storms. Her colleague, Angel, joined us, sharing her own story of loss and renewal. Three women, spanning different generations, finding solace in unexpected sanctuary.

When Jackson finally wrapped his arms around my legs Saturday evening, I knelt to his level. 'Nan so long?'

Nan, What Took You So Long?

I smiled, smoothing his unruly hair. 'Well, little man, Nan met some people who needed hugs along the way. And you know what? Sometimes the best part of coming home is the journey that teaches you why home matters so much.'

His wide eyes studied my face seriously, then he nodded with the wisdom only toddlers possess. 'Okay, Nan. Here now.'

Indeed I was. And I was exactly where I belonged.

Babies are Still Dangerous

E Taylor

At the supermarket, she is happy to find that frozen duck is $10 on special. She is thrilled at the bargain. She plans to braise it whole and looks forward to cooking it for the family tomorrow. How surprising. She hasn't felt joy in a long time.

Although sadness no longer incapacitates her, she had recently been reminded that babies are still dangerous. It happened when she had held a young woman's baby. The baby looked up at her, his eyes like deep pools of water. Trusting. Happy.

Immediately, it transported her back to when her children were little. She had known when they were afraid, or hungry, or tired; and she could do something about it. But they grew up. She and her husband had done their best to build a Christian home full of love. Her mistake was to think that this would shield their children from the pain and brokenness of this world. Now that her children are young adults, things are quieter, calmer. But as she looked at that beautiful baby boy, a wave of sorrow surged up and knocked emotional composure right out of her. She had handed the baby back to his mother, and turned to wipe away a tear.

The next day, she cooks the duck, rendering off the fat till the skin turns golden, then braising it whole, with aromatics and spices. Cooking was one thing that she and her son used to enjoy together. She had always pushed back against gender stereotyping: why shouldn't boys cook or sing or sew? But as time passed, she too had wondered.

Babies are Still Dangerous

One day, she opened up to him, 'You know I've never enjoyed shopping for clothes or wearing make-up. I've often felt different.' It was an invitation for him to speak. And he had spoken.

'Mum, I'm gay.'

In the months following this revelation, she couldn't bear to look at old childhood photographs, which captured so many happy memories. It felt as if that word 'gay' had stolen everything: all beauty from the past, all hope for the future. Had she loved him too much? Had she made him gay?

It became her secret and she would wince when people made gay jokes. 'If only you knew,' she would think to herself, 'in our family, it's no longer us and them. It's us and us.' But she knew that their intact family was something to be treasured. The revelation hadn't divided them. They still had one another, and some of them still had God.

In the evening, the family sit down to dinner. She has jointed the duck and arranged every piece on the platter, beautifully presented beside some vibrant Asian greens. Some of them enjoy the meaty pieces, while others prefer to pick slivers off the bone.

She used to complain about the amount of time spent around food: shopping, cooking, washing up. Now she thanks God for the gift of cooking: such an uncomplicated way to show love, and so much pleasure to be had in eating together.

'Thanks, Mum. That was good,' says her son. He is right. It is good.

As time passes, she sees her son's revelation not as an invalidation of the past, but as an invitation to a deeper connection with him, to know him more fully. The past was not a lie, but her understanding of so much had been incomplete. She comes to rest in the assurance that the revelation didn't catch God by surprise. The God-who-had-known walks with her into the unknown.

As she is able, she accepts her son's invitation. She starts to enjoy his company again, starts to appreciate his talents again, and starts to get to know his other friends. She doesn't know this yet, but one day in the not-so-distant future, she will be able to hold other people's babies without crying.

Another Ordinary Day

Karen Roper

It was just another ordinary weekday. Another day of catching the train to work, working all day and then catching the train home. Nothing exciting ever seemed to happen – it was just an ordinary day.

Standing at the train station that morning with all the other commuters, with the sun barely peeking through the clouds, this is what it felt like. Just ordinary. The electric train rumbled into the station, I got on and went to sit in my favourite seat. As the journey took a little under one hour, it was important to get comfortable. I hung one bag over the armrest and put the other on my lap and then searched in my lap bag for my e-reader and my devotion book.

Turning to the date in the devotion book and, opening my Bible on the e-reader, I began to read the Word of God as was my habit first thing on the morning train.

The train rumbled along and stopped to pick up more passengers and let a few off. The regular announcement, 'Doors closing; please stand clear,' faded into the background after a while. As I looked up from my reading and glanced around the train, I could see some getting a little more sleep, others reading a book, talking quietly or still others just looking out the windows. Some of these people I had seen over and over on my morning commute whilst others I hadn't seen before. Nobody was really paying attention to anyone else. It was quiet except for the train conductor's voice announcing each station as we came into it, the sound of the doors opening and closing at each station and that irritating, repetitive announcement about the doors closing.

After finishing my morning Bible reading and my devotion, I put the e-reader and devotion book back and then rummaged in my bag to find the latest Christian magazine I had received in the mail.

The train was still doing its thing – stopping at stations and picking up even more passengers. I looked around and noticed the train getting quite full.

I opened the magazine and started to read. All of a sudden, I heard a voice: 'Excuse me, are you reading a Christian magazine?'

I looked up to see where the voice was coming from, and it was the lady sitting directly opposite me. I had never seen her before. She was middle-aged and had her eyes fixed on me – eyes that were full of curiosity.

'Yes,' I stated unsurely. I didn't know what to make of the question. Where was this conversation going to lead?

She then said, 'I have noticed you reading it for a while, a couple of days, and wanted to ask you some questions.'

'Okay,' I stammered, wondering whether I was going to be able to answer her sufficiently and with what God wanted me to say. 'Help, God,' I whispered quietly.

'I have been having some troubles lately and wondered if God still heard me,' she whispered.

'Oh yes,' I said more confidently.

For the next twenty minutes as we sat there on the train, two strangers, she poured out her heart to me while I listened and offered her what the Word of God said.

I could see the hope building up on her face and the fact that God was ministering to her right there on that crowded train.

Another Ordinary Day

My station was coming up where I needed to get off to go to work. I told her this and she said that it was her station too.

As we packed our bags and pulled our train tickets out of our purses, we stood up together. We both got off the train.

We chatted for a bit and then I said, 'Can I pray for you?'

She said, 'Of course.'

So we stood there on a crowded train platform, with passengers going every which way, with our hands held, praying and asking God for His wisdom, His guidance and His direction. Tears were rolling down both of our faces at this point.

When I said, 'Amen,' we hugged each other and went our separate ways. As I rode up the escalator and walked out of the train station to work, I marvelled at the way that God uses the ordinary to create an extraordinary moment. Who would have thought that reading a Christian magazine on a train would witness to anybody? But God uses those seemingly insignificant moments to do the work in others' lives that we don't expect.

I caught the same train and sat in the same carriage, but I never did see that lady again. I still wonder what has transpired in her life.

When Despair for the World Grows in Me
After *The Peace of Wild Things* by Wendell Berry
Tamara Harpford

In this wilding world as pompous weeds choke the hope of merciful folk, in which fear takes root over the carcases of buried books, fertilised with othering, I wake.

Usually I lie, uneasy, and prepare my excuses for a despair-affected day…but from a poem crafted in tribute to Grace, I remember there is another way. I flip the bedsheets from my overheating worry and welcome the cool shock of clear air. In a strange bout of sanity, I pull on comfort clothes and grab the cold car keys from their hook.

There's a pond and I must go there.

I pack my heavy fight and anger so I can toss them into the dark pool amongst the frogs and the mosquito wrigglers and the rotting leaf litter.

When I arrive, at first there's just the rush of stormwater through a drain – an earlier deluge had started cleaning up the greasy streets. As I sit on a slippery log beside the pond I hear the whispers of bin-chicken wings and plover barks and koala grunts, and the reeds' dancing rustle.

There are duck discos in the hours before dawn – who knew?

I ask the ducks if they're afraid, but they don't reply except to utter a thanks to their Eternal Maker, and dance and dive and eat their fill from around the weeds and the reeds. It's not ignorance; it's trust.

I look up, and above a break in the tree canopy opens a break in the clouds, and a solitary star shines through. It winks at me from its seat in the heavenly choir stalls, beyond the present storm.

When Despair for the World Grows in Me

Somewhere amongst the grey clouds in my head, there is a breath, a rest, a reset. Despair has flown. Around my brow, a nest of grace, woven through with light threads of wariness.

My fight and anger have shrivelled like tea leaves. I carry them home again. I might need them another day.

An 'Ordinary' Faith

Lexia G Mackin

The dust was red. The land was as flat as a table. And there was one mountain in the whole of the landscape, between us and the coastal strip of Western Australia. There was one highway, if you could call a single lane road a highway, that travelled north to south. Along this highway, there were places of interest: Port Hedland, Roebourne, Carnarvon, Geraldton, but with nothing in-between unless you were a local and knew the places that were off the beaten track.

We had spent four wonderful days camping at Wittenoom, in the Hammersley Ranges in Western Australia, with fellow believers over the Easter weekend, talking about matters of faith, life, and children. With five children in tow, it didn't matter for once in their life if they didn't wash their hands before eating, that their feet were always dirty (there was always Joffre Creek), and it didn't matter that I always sheltered my cup of tea with my hand to stop the flies from thinking my cuppa was their private jacuzzi.

Being 'Mr nuts and bolts' man, my husband took meticulous care of his pride and joy, a blue HG Premier V8 Holden station wagon. He checked the water in the radiator, made sure the hoses (somewhere under the bonnet) didn't have any leaks, pumped the tyres, and was ready to begin the four and a half hour journey ahead of him, wife and five children in tow.

But there was a problem: one of the tyres was scrubbing on the inside mudguard. We were the last of the convoy to depart so, after a quick time of prayer, we decided to begin the journey. I made sure that we had water for the car and water for the children in case we were stranded on the side of the road for any length of time. The day-time temperatures at this time of year could easily reach 48-60 degrees Celsius, so we had to be

An 'Ordinary' Faith

prepared. We also had numerous books and games to keep the children occupied on the journey. Having recently experienced the joy of the Holy Spirit, we knew we could conquer anything.

As we travelled up this one solitary mountain, the offending tyre began to protest loudly, getting louder and louder by the minute. We knew we had a serious problem on our hands but didn't quite know what it was. Each side of the mountain, with its steep drop below, took on a sinister aspect. But with our faith in the Holy Spirit and the V8 engine, we powered on. As we continued, I sat in a state of quiet expectation. We were on an adventure with the Holy Spirit.

We finally came down onto the flat of the countryside and the tyre got steadily worse. The noise was now a grating sound that began to alarm the children in the back of the station wagon. At this point, I should also mention that we were towing a 22-foot caravan behind us. A rare sight so far away from suburbia.

Sharing Easter with us were two bus loads of about sixty Aboriginal children, some from local boarding schools in Roebourne and Port Hedland, along with families from the Roebourne and Port Hedland fellowships.

As we powered on past the buses, many heads and hands out the window, smiling faces and screeching voices greeted us. We honked our horn in response and created a joyous camaraderie between the children of the bus and our children in the car.

We had arranged with those who had left before us to take a slight detour and stop off at the bottom of a small waterfall that cascaded into a decent pond at the bottom. Water was scarce in the north west of Western Australia so a swim in Python Pool was to be one of the highlights of the weekend. As we pulled in to park the car and van, my sense of expectation kept growing. I explained this to my husband and, after a quick prayer, we decided we should continue our journey and get ahead of the bus we knew to be following us, although we didn't know why.

Several miles down the road (we measured distance in miles back then), we could no longer ignore the noise of the tyre. We pulled up along the side of the road and waited for the bus to arrive. There was no other traffic on the road so I set out to entertain the children while we waited, keeping silent vigil in my spirit to the leading of the Spirit of God.

It took over a half hour to explain our situation and then get the caravan hooked up to the back of the bus. That was a sight! A bus towing a caravan. My husband's brother, who was travelling with the children on the bus, offered to travel in the car with my husband while I travelled on the bus with my children and around thirty Aboriginal children. Apparently, I wasn't the only one who was excited but I think my excitement sprang from a different source. What a noise!

My two young boys joined the other boys at the back of the bus and the teenage girls took my toddler and entertained her all the way home, the other children somewhere in between. They were fascinated with my toddler's fine blonde hair and, between clapping games and laughter, they kept touching her hair and giggling. Bereft of children to look after, I only had to suffer through the overwhelming noise of so many excited children and the bumpy paved roads.

We made it home to Roebourne safely. I bathed and fed the children, put them to bed, and then tried to recount the story of our journey to our house sitters. Being American, they were fascinated with life in remote Australia.

An 'Ordinary' Faith

As I was telling the part where I left my husband and brother-in-law on the side of the road, my neighbour from across the road ran out of his house, jumped into the ambulance parked in his driveway and drove away at great speed.

In true story-teller mode, I blithely said, 'Oh, look. There's Tom. He's probably going to my husband now. I wonder what's happened.' Dumbfounded doesn't even begin to describe the looks on their faces. I tried to tell them that, with the extra dimension of the Holy Spirit now in our lives, I didn't have any sense of trauma and, therefore, of alarm. Well, you could see that they thought I just didn't have any sense, full stop!

What I didn't know until later was that, at the same moment, my husband was in the home of the local tow truck driver, trying to organise a tow for our car. On the CB radio, they both heard the local police requesting his assistance for a stranded HG Holden station wagon that had been left outside the local speedway. My husband and brother-in-law had managed to get the car within ten kilometres of home before the offending wheel and axle had finally, and completely, worked its way out of the differential. Hubby managed to get a lift to the tow truck driver's house for assistance, leaving my brother-in-law at the scene to warn other drivers of the now quite dead Pride and Joy.

The adventure with the Holy Spirit continued. Another layer of excitement was added to our story by the police in Roebourne. They were tailing a young man who was quite inebriated but, for some reason, weren't able to arrest him until he had committed a driving offence, which they were sure was about to happen.

By the time the Keystone Cops car chase had neared the speedway, the inebriated driver was looking in his rear-vision mirror so much he failed to see the dead Pride and Joy on the side of the road. He also failed to see my brother-in-law's torch light as it bobbed its way through the spinifex grasses, running away from the driver's trajectory, and he ran straight into the back of our car. Now I should mention that his car was quite a bit more expensive than ours. It was a 1976 Ford LTD – his Pride and Joy.

The end of the story? Well, with the Holy Spirit's prompting, I knew the adventure wasn't finished. Our car, now totally written off, was only fit for spare parts; our family had no method of transport (there was no such thing as public transport in our area); and we had no insurance because we believed God was our sole source of supply and would look after us. Blind faith. Yes, but justified.

Two weeks later, we heard a knock on the front door. The inebriated driver, now quite sobered from his experience, handed us, in cash, the value of our car. I knew, then, that blind faith, when put into the hands of a holy and loving God, was to be our new ordinary.

Happy Caterpillar Smiles

Diana Davison

The last festive season didn't provide many highlights for me. I spent December, Christmas and the New Year period moving possessions out of our Gold Coast apartment. The whole affair was tense, tiring, and not without the occasional private tear. The decision to sell our holiday home had been bubbling for a long while. It became necessary to implement action.

Unfortunately, further down the track in early March, Cyclone Alfred came knocking. An uninvited guest and an unforeseen challenge to dampen spirits. All occurring while I was overseas, leaving my husband to pick up the pieces and liaise with tradespeople. But we were not the only coastal residents to experience streams of property damage. We paused the sale to reassess and repair. Flooded floor boards, leaks in the ceiling, shattered pool fence, detached storage cupboard doors outside all required troubleshooting and insurance assessed.

And so the year's first quarter took its toll. Everything – my journey, family, writing projects and general wellbeing – seemed uncertain, up in the air in a holding pattern.

Once returned to Brisbane, I phone my Sydney-based friend, Lesley, and my valued prayer partner. We pray together over our mobile phones and across states, asking for guidance and clarity and that all would soon revert to normal. Happiness and harmony are both crucial components to my existence.

The next morning, I'm compelled to seize a much needed walk out in the open. I pull up in my car at the local park. When I arrive, I see a procession of young green-uniformed primary school kids. They travel in a line like a caterpillar, meandering with enthusiasm. The vibrant pink colour of my ride instantly grabs their attention. They are walking single and double file with two teachers flanking either end. But the look on each face is priceless, making up for the heaviness of my mood.

Every child turns in my direction as I sit behind the wheel. Each youngster presents me with a wide smile and waves, in junior salute fashion, as they all proceed by. Lucky for me to be there at that precise juncture to receive such a welcome. The scene moves me. It is the boost I had sought and they unwittingly gift it to me. Such an 'aww' moment. So innocent. So unexpected.

'Thank you for this beautiful acknowledgment,' I voice quietly. The delightful facial expressions of all the children prompt me to recognise the importance of nature and the joys of being.

On that radiant sunny day, I knew I was not alone. I received answers to my preoccupations and prayers, revealed in a way I clearly understand. That incident serves a reminder to take a step back and enjoy the simple pleasures of life. Goodness is in abundance and exists all around us, always on hand to help bring balance and blessings. It is the essence so easily ignored, yet right under our very noses.

Blowing Balloons May be Hazardous to Your Health

Anusha Atukorala

It's been a long journey – this uphill trek with severe pain and debilitating fatigue. I'm sick of being sick! God asks me to continue to wait on Him for my healing from chronic illness. Unfortunately…patience is not my strong point. Perhaps to help me in the patience department, I was given an unexpected gift recently; a six week trip into the unknown.

My GP discovered a murmur in my heart and sent me for a scan. As I lay there, chatting to a friendly technician, a supernatural peace flooded my being – God was letting me know that I would be fine. At first, I assumed that the scan would show nothing was wrong with my heart. But…as I witnessed the flurry of activity around me, I knew there was something terribly amiss.

I realised then what the peace meant – that although things may look concerning, eventually, all would be well. Anxiety often pokes me at the drop of hat, so the calm I felt *had* to be God!

I was told that I had a heart disorder that could turn fatal in certain conditions. Even blowing balloons could lead to sudden death. Fancy that! I was sent for a battery of expensive tests. I didn't know then if I'd go through months or years of hardship. I just knew that God had indicated that it would *eventually* turn out fine. And so, I was able to smile through it all, secure in His love for me. As I spent the next few weeks having a myriad of tests completed, His perfect peace guarded my heart.

Six weeks later, when I went back to the cardiologist, I didn't know what to expect, so braced myself for bad news. The first bit of good news was that my heart had no arrhythmias. Hooray! The next piece of news was that my arteries had ZERO calcification. Not bad for a lady in her sizzling sixties! But wait. There was more. The final good news was that I didn't have a nasty heart condition which had been suspected. The best news, therefore, was that no open heart surgery would be required. *Whew*! Thank You, Jesus.

My original diagnosis still exists but the news was much better than I could have hoped for. Best of all was the surreal peace that had been my impeccable attire right through. It was the first time that God had given me a peace that passed all understanding *before* a trial began.

I still need to be careful – no blowing balloons for me. But as I continue my journey into good health, all I've encountered with Jesus in my recent past opens a window for the healing yet to come. And now hope shines bright, a candle glowing in the darkness, because this unexpected experience has caused my faith to grow. God surely proved to me that He's in control, a faithful, loving heavenly Father whom I can trust with all my heart.

A House for Fay

Jo Wanmer

Fay needed a house, her third since I'd met her about two years ago. Following the 9/11 disaster, rentals were hard to find, even harder for a single woman who was pregnant with her seventh baby.

I encouraged her to write a list of things she'd like in a home. We laid it before God, prayed, and believed He could do it.

Weeks passed. She managed to get a month's extension on her current house. Everywhere she applied turned her down.

We prayed again…for anything. 'Lord, these little ones need a home.' Praying in my bed one night, God interrupted—'You buy her a house.'

Stunned, I ignored the thought and dismissed it. But it persisted.

'Lord, have you seen our bank balance?' No reply.

'Lord, it's impossible.' No reply.

It seems God didn't have to justify His instructions. Pushing aside my nervousness, I interrupted Steve at work to explain what I thought God had said. I expected him to tell me to stop such silliness and forget it.

He leant back in his chair. 'Let me think…I know a bloke who could help you.' He handed me a business card. 'Ring him.'

Hands shaking, I dialled the number and made an appointment. After poring over our figures, and scribbling in his book, he looked up. 'It's possible. Your budget is tight. However, we can try.'

Rereading Fay's list, I panicked. How easy it had been to suggest she have faith. Now I needed to buy a house that included five bedrooms, a swimming pool, a sand pit, and a rainwater tank, all on a minimum budget. My turn to walk in faith, a very shaky faith.

This helpful man took me to many houses. None of them could accommodate her family, no matter how we tried.

After two days, I thanked him for helping me with this wild-goose chase. I returned to prayer. 'Lord, Fay needs a house. Urgently.'

The same thought persisted. 'You buy her a house.'

'I've tried. There's nothing.' No reply

I sighed. 'Please lead us.'

We entered a pretty home in a great location. Could this be the one? It was small inside but had four bedrooms with a corner where a fifth had been removed.

Encouraged, I asked, 'Is this it, Lord?' His reply became obvious once I explored the back yard. It had a great garden, an above-ground pool, a small rainwater tank and even a fenced sand pit. A separate double garage, other sheds and an entertainment area were bonuses.

Stunned by this beautiful haven that could comfortably accommodate Fay and her family, I bought it, praising God. That afternoon I again interrupted Steve at his desk. 'We found it…or God found it. Just sign here.'

He grinned. 'Thank you, Lord.' Without question or hesitation he signed the documents, agreeing to two mortgages.

I rang Fay. 'We found your home!'

Weeks later as I perused final documents after purchasing the house, I discovered our total remaining balance in the bank account was five cents!

Seeing the Sparkle through Tears

Karen Curran

'I wish it were me instead of you, Karen,' Mother said, her voice breaking. I sat in a chair, not speaking, phone pressed to my ear.

I had just learned I had breast cancer and my mind was numb. The doctor had suggested two options: mastectomy, or lumpectomy followed by radiation. This news came one month after I had cancelled a 25-year-old cancer insurance policy that covered surgery, chemotherapy, and radiation, believing there had to be a healthier way to treat this dreaded disease.

Somehow my mind now seemed willing to consider any option, even without the extra insurance coverage.

I had lived as a health fanatic for the previous five years, eating healthy meals, exercising relentlessly, and feeding my family veggie burgers. I was studying to become a Doctor of Naturopathy and expected to be a shining example of health in the practice I planned to open.

Life was good. With a wonderful husband and kids, I had solid plans for the future. My mom and I only saw each other two to three times a year, but the telephone worked well for sharing family stories. We enjoyed laughing together, whether it was about a silly thing someone said, or over my son's insistence that my parents were like the Energizer Bunny because, though they were in their seventies, they kept going – and going – and going.

Mother had survived almost every surgery imaginable: heart, spinal, thyroid, gall bladder, hysterectomy, and had always made a recovery that allowed her to resume her active lifestyle. I, too, almost wished she was facing cancer rather than me, since she had such an incredible record of bouncing back.

I chose the lumpectomy/radiation option though it was contrary to everything I believed about cancer treatment. After much prayer, George and I felt it was the path to follow. But I felt no peace, only anger.

During my first visit to the radiation treatment centre, I lay quietly on the table while the radiation technician took necessary measurements. The technician, Shirley, spoke softly, explaining every step. I didn't respond, bound in rigid silence. When she finished, we didn't speak as I was dressing. But then Shirley stepped towards me.

'I know you're afraid,' she said.

'I'm not afraid,' I exploded. 'I'm angry! I'm a healthy person. This shouldn't be happening to me.'

Thoughtfully, Shirley took my hands in hers and gazed into my eyes. After a moment, she said, 'Just remember – we have a Saviour.' As I dissolved into tears, Shirley put her arms around me. She didn't say anything else, nor did she need to. I had heard what I needed to hear. My focus turned to God, where it should have been all along. I slowly began to relinquish my health to His very capable hands.

Two weeks into my therapy, I learned that Mother had decided to go ahead with the heart valve replacement surgery she'd anticipated for years.

'You don't need to be here, Karen,' she said. 'You can't miss your treatments. Besides, your sister plans to come and, of course, your daddy is here. I'll be fine.' Still, she insisted on saying goodbye to each member of my family. I should have realised…

Seeing the Sparkle through Tears

Mother didn't survive the surgery. Her heart simply fell apart and even thirteen hours of surgery couldn't put it together again. She had always been vibrant and alive and I had missed the chance to hug her and have my day brightened by the sparkle in her blue eyes. How could any cancer treatment have been more important than that?

I went to the cancer centre the morning before my flight home for the funeral and was called from the waiting room by Shirley, the technician I had not seen since my initial visit.

'Shirley,' I said, 'you were a blessing to me that first day when you reminded me of my Saviour.' She simply smiled. When I told her that I needed to be reminded again since my mother had just died, Shirley took me in her arms. We stood in the hallway and cried together. When we reached the treatment room, she said, 'Let's pray.' Shirley, the other technician and I stood close together holding hands as Shirley prayed. Minutes later, I sat in an examination room waiting to see the doctor since I needed to discuss possible consequences for missing treatments while I was away. For most of our meeting, though, my kind doctor sat with me and held my hand as we talked about my mother.

I was loved that day by my Christian technicians and nurses, and by my Jewish doctor. But most of all, I was loved by God. He reminded me, through His people, that He is present and that He loves me. He reassured me that He is in control even when we don't understand the things that are happening. And He showed me that I can treasure and enjoy the past, even as I continue to make new memories.

As I choose to appreciate my blessings, I can almost see the sparkle as God – and Mother – smile down at me.

Crying Help
Phil Bell

When I was a boy
I almost floated out to sea,
because there was no way I was going to cry for help
while I still had a toehold on the sand,
at least in between the waves.

This was a proud determination that I kept to
all the rebel years of my youth – I would be responsible
for keeping my own head above water.

Coming to the end of myself was a hard road,
but I thought I short-cut it pretty well
by changing paths when things became too bumpy,
hitching myself to Jesus and his ways.

It's sad that over time that walk with Jesus,
with all its joys,
could be so painfully corrupted
by that original heart determination – the idea that somehow
by getting my act together
I could make it all go right,
could pull myself out of my disappointments and my self-comforts,

Crying Help

could save myself
even as the rising tide threatened to sweep me away.

Rescue was always at hand.

For the boy in the waves it came from my dad,
alerted by the unselfconscious shouts
  of another child caught in the same riptide.

For the older me,
I didn't receive my rescue
until I gave up on my silence,
opened my heart to some fellow travellers,
and actually called for help.

Wheels of Change

Jo Wanmer

Clickety-clack. Clickety-clack. The train wheels clattered through the night. I tossed on the hard bunk, sleep pushed aside by questions without answers. I'd travelled on this train to boarding school before. School would be the same but I was different. How did the different me fit in? What would I say to my friends?

Three weeks before the holidays, I'd left school in a rush. Called out of class by Jacko, the head mistress. 'Your Dad has suffered a heart attack and your mother needs you at home to help.' She nodded her head, her cheeks wobbling like jelly.

'Dad! Is he okay?'

'He'll be fine. Don't go back to class. Go and pack. Someone is coming to take you to the airport.' With a wave of her hand, I was dismissed.

Upstairs I flopped on the edge of my bed. Airport! I'd never been on a plane. Dazed, I threw things in my bag and waited downstairs for a man I'd never met. *God, Dad must be okay. He just must.*

On the plane, my sister, an uncle and an aunt were already seated. My world bottomed out. I quelled tears and tried to calm my stomach as the small plane bounced through the sky.

The next three weeks were a roller coaster of emotions. Most days we drove to see Dad in the little local hospital. The excitement of house visitors and the buzz of being home enlivened me. Niggling doubt about Dad's recovery lay over us like a cloud. The drawn look on my mother's face reminded me everything was changing.

Wheels of Change

On the day the sky was weeping, we couldn't traverse the dirt roads to visit Dad. He was looking much better anyway. Most other relatives had returned home. Conversations now focused on life when Dad came home. Engaged in the ordinary, we were interrupted by a vehicle – a rare occurrence on our road. On the front veranda, we waited to greet the car. A council truck, equipped to handle mud, slipped up the road. A passenger sat sombre-faced. Our minister. As soon as Mum saw him, her hands flew to her face. 'Oh, no. Lord, no.'

She'd understood correctly. Dad had been found dead in his bed.

Then the whole world was weeping.

The next hours were a battle between denial and reality. Dad wouldn't be home. Ever. The council truck drove me to my brother who was working with our farm hand. They stopped and listened, eyes wide, as I relayed the news.

Days flew by. The phone rang often. The post office lady would simply say. 'I have more telegrams. Are you ready to write them down?' They came about eight at a time. An outpouring of grief from hundreds of people who were as shocked as we. These simple messages comforted our hearts.

Family members who had left, along with others, flew to be with us. Friends met the planes and drove them to our place. Somewhere we found beds. My mother did need me. I watched her go through the motions but the spark of life had left, leaving her washed-out, grey.

At the funeral, people crowded everywhere, inside and out of our little country church. The procession to the cemetery passed my old school where every student lined the fence. I wondered if anyone was counting the cars as I had always done.

Abruptly the busyness was over, the visitors gone. A new normal had to be found. So I hugged my grey mother and I lay in a train in the dead of night listening to the clickety-clack and wondering if I knew how to be me.

My old group of friends shrank in embarrassment or became tongue-tied around me. We didn't share a language for this unknown. But some of the other girls gathered me in. Girls I hadn't known well. Worldly girls whose conversation covered things I had been sheltered from. But girls who'd had plenty of knocks in life, who understood grief.

Their unconditional acceptance of me, their ability to make me laugh, their understanding of deep, breath-stealing heart pain, enabled me to re engage into school. It was different, as was everything.

Clickety-clack. Clickety-clack. The wheels sounded more positive on the way home for the Christmas holidays. A friend talked me into dyeing our hair with magic silver white in the tiny basin on the train. We emerged from the carriage laughing, with purple hair and purple fingers. A grey shadow of my mother hugged me.

But now, living in a home without Dad, reality slammed into me. To learn of the decision to sell our property, the only home I'd ever known, ripped the guts out of me. Mum showed me our new house. She'd bought the ugliest house in town. It mortified me. Fibro-clad in and out, it had never been painted and so was the ugly, aged brown of weathered cladding.

But I was my father's daughter. Trained to be resilient, to find a way, to stand on my own two feet. Soon my younger brother and I descended on that house, armed with paint and rollers, lots of determination and very little practical knowledge. This little three bedder's inside walls changed from aged-fibro-grey to the fresher grey my faded-out Mum had chosen. No-one told us that old fibro drinks paint like a camel at a water trough. We were often frustrated by running out of paint until someone told us to add water. And we struggled to find a lift to town. Why did we need a lift? Old enough to paint an entire house by ourselves, but neither of us were old enough to obtain a car licence.

Christmas without Dad must have happened. I don't have any recollection, but too soon I was back on the dark bunk listening to the clickety-clack of the world's slowest train. My final year of school awaited me. For the last time, I'd farewelled the property where I'd lived, played and worked. I'd left the only house I'd ever known, my siblings and my grey mother. This year I was compelled to excel because that's what Dad wanted, and whether he was dead or alive, as always, I wanted to please him. Even if I didn't get to see the proud glint in his eye and feel the swift gentle hug, I could still imagine.

At boarding school, after dinner, we were ushered into a classroom to study. Saturdays we all wrote letters home. Mum's letters still arrived twice a week but they had lost their interest and sparkle.

After the next train ride, Mum met me and took me 'home'. In reality she took me to the ugly house. She'd squashed three beds into one room for her three daughters. My older sister worked in Brisbane and wasn't home often. My younger sister was five. I felt as though I was invading her space, as though I had no space. I welcomed the clickety-clack of the wheels through the night when I returned, as now school felt more familiar than home.

Grief is an unpredictable animal. It would hit in the middle of a movie, or when I was asked to lead chapel, or in the dead of night. My friend who'd helped me dye my hair approached the stern, unapproachable, unpredictable Jacko, expressing her concerns about me. Jacko invited us to go out for a picnic while she visited family. To leave the school was rare. With a packed picnic basket, she left us to rest on green grass under trees. She, too, must have understood grief to give me such a precious gift.

Exams done, school finished, hats thrown and school shirts signed, Mum drove me home, excited to show me the house, now with exterior paint. No longer the ugliest house in town. Even she had a little more life, a little more colour.

Clickety-clack. Clickety-clack. A longer trip with no school friends, all alone. This train took me to Brisbane to a girl's college, and then to tackle the University of Queensland. If Dad had been alive, he would have accompanied me. But he wasn't. Mum was sure that my self-sufficiency would enable me to master all these unknowns, and I did. Within days I was hitching a ride along Coronation Drive like the rest of the girls.

Who was I? As we were pushed and pulled by lobby groups, it became obvious that decisions made now would affect the rest of my life. Knowing my dad's eye was on me, and that Mum was praying for me, kept me on the path I'd been trained in. But I was different. When I came across people in pain, I could relate to them.

In life Dad taught me many things, impressed life skills on me, taught me about God. In death, he taught me to be strong, walk my own path, make good decisions and love those who were hurting, because now I understood deep pain and loss.

'But That's a Cult…'

R J Rodda

After being a very ordinary girl from a small country town in Australia, I loved the rush of being in Tokyo. I revelled in being jammed next to strangers in trains and slurping ramen at the noodle bars. But after three months I started to long for more than the life of a working tourist. I identified my Japanese church as the problem.

It was actually a great church. I had been brought there by my aunt's friend Stephen, a blond-haired, intelligent Australian man. He went there, along with his Japanese wife, and a handful of other older ex-pats. But there was one significant difference between those foreigners and me – they understood Japanese. I did not. And the service was all in Japanese.

So I would attempt to sing the songs and sit during the sermon with my paper dictionary, trying to catch a word here or there that I could look up. Occasionally Stephen or another foreigner would offer me a whispered translation, but by the end of three months I felt very dry spiritually and a strong desire came over me to find a church where the service was in English. I hungered to be spiritually nourished in a language I understood and I wanted to make real Christian friends I could communicate with that were my age.

At this key, vulnerable time, I bumped into Amanda, a tall American girl with broad shoulders and long straight honey-coloured hair. She stopped when she saw me on the street and approached me with a warm smile. I smiled back, disarmed by her friendliness. And almost straight away she mentioned Jesus. I was surprised by this, and even had a twinge of guilt. I was never that quick to mention my faith straight off to a stranger, but I mentioned that yes, I too believed in Jesus and went to church.

Turning Ten and other stories of life

Her response was to invite me to *her* church, which had a familiar and trustworthy name (she did not tell me the actual full name of the church at that time). When Amanda added that her church service was in English, I decided to go.

Before church, she invited me to her small apartment where I met her flatmates. They all talked about Jesus and were very friendly. My telephone became crowded with their numbers. Far away from home and the church I had grown up in, had I found a replacement Christian family?

Their church building was like a piece of modern art in a prime location in Tokyo. The main difference I noticed from other churches I'd been to was that the choir at the front sang *a cappella* throughout. I realised the church was probably anti-instruments, but decided that it was an unimportant stylistic difference. I was so keen to be one of them, I didn't see any red flags. Afterwards I was greeted by a number of people who seemed genuinely interested in me. I had never been so instantly embraced or so swiftly included in any setting, and in a foreign country where I was naturally on the outer, this was intoxicating.

Then Amanda invited me to do a Bible Talk with her and a friend that night. I refused, went home, and began praying about it. I'm not the kind of person who occasionally visits a church. Did God want me to commit to going? It was silly, perhaps, but I felt somewhat uneasy about their dedication. They were so passionate in proclaiming Jesus. Why did their intensity make me feel uncomfortable? Was it because I was holding back from God in some fundamental way, that the thought of going all-out frightened me?

As I prayed, I felt like God told me he wanted me to go to their church. I texted Amanda, telling her I would come the following Sunday and do a Bible Talk with her and her friend afterwards.

'But That's a Cult...'

That Sunday, several hours before I needed to leave, my aunt's friend Stephen rang me about something trivial. He had never rung me before. (He never rang me again.) And for some reason, I blurted out that I was going to this new church that evening.

'But that's a cult,' Stephen spluttered. 'If that's the one I've heard about, it's a cult.' This alarmed me, but I told him I'd promised all these very nice people, my new friends, that I would go. I didn't want to break my word if he didn't know for sure it was a cult. He must be wrong. People in a cult didn't talk about Jesus, right?

Still very concerned, Stephen offered to come with me. His home was far away but he must have dropped everything to arrive in time to accompany me up those stairs into the church. By the time of the closing song, Stephen, with a solemn face, indicated that we should leave. On the way out we were greeted by people with huge smiles, all saying how 'impacted' they were by God and how great their lives were now. They were not interested in hearing about my faith experiences or Stephen's, only in talking about their own.

Afterwards, Stephen sat me down and explained to me that the church was definitely a cult. My heart plunged into a cold fright. I'd been so close to joining. So close to enmeshing myself with them. Stephen said that a healthy church has people in it of all age ranges. A cult had people that were all the same – in this case they were all young adult professional types. There were no old people or children. The sermon too, although it mentioned Jesus in slogans, focused on praising different people, who were pointed out one by one and clapped for being successful at bringing 'people to Christ', that is, bringing people into this church. There was no actual focus on reading the Bible and discussing what it says. Stephen also told me he'd heard the Bible Talks were about making you confess your sins to them and then they'd used this to pressure you to join their church, even if you were a member of another (a quick Google search confirmed this – why hadn't I checked Google before this?).

I came away both humbled by the experience and astounded by the mercy of God. I'd prayed to God, genuinely seeking His will. I thought He'd told me to go to that church. I'd heard wrong. But God did not leave me to blunder off into a web of very sincere, very relentless people whom I would have found it very difficult to politely refuse. Instead, he sent me Stephen whose words gave me the courage to block all the new numbers on my phone.

Stephen then took me to a new, Bible-believing church that was in both Japanese and English. It was not as friendly as the cult – real churches aren't – but it had lots of different types of people: old, young, Japanese, Korean, American, and people my age who spoke my language. I became refreshed spiritually and, over time, made genuine life-changing friendships that enriched my stay in Tokyo and gave me what I was most longing for. A family away from home.

An Unrelenting Love

Brock Meier

Although I was not mindful of the fact, this day would have been our 43rd wedding anniversary. But the agonising and final rupture of divorce had ended our marriage after my ex-wife left home eighteen months earlier. I determined this day to go through a final stack of papers and such – one of many stacks she had left me in the back bedroom, the location she had been using to store my things that she had divided from hers. The stack held a wide-ranging variety of ancient receipts, notes I'd written, and old to-do lists.

Thumbing through the miscellany of papers, I came upon a collection of old greeting cards. They were from my parents, our daughter and, most poignant of all, from my former wife. Birthday cards, Valentine's Day cards, and cards simply declaring her friendship and love for me, acknowledging that while our lives together had been difficult, she had renewed hope we could endure. These cards undid me. Reading through them, I wept.

I finished the job I'd been determined to do, but my heart capsized. Well into the stack, I came across a 3-inch square, printed piece of paper. On it were the lyrics of an old hymn: 'O Love That Will Not Let Me Go.' I had first heard the song six or seven years previous, and its lyrics so captured my heart that I typed them up and printed them out so I could remember them. That was probably the last time I saw the piece of paper before I dug it out of the stack this day. Though I still believed the song's words, it didn't change my sadness to joy. I took the paper and laid it prominently on my kitchen table, so I would see it often and reflect upon the words.

Later in the day, a dear and longtime friend texted me, asking how I was. I mentioned sorting through the last stack of stuff my wife had left me, and how the old cards had hit me hard (I didn't mention finding the song). But I also said how, not long after the sadness swept over me, two friends had independently and unexpectedly shown up on my doorstep, though it was in the midst of the initial COVID panic. I texted my friend: 'It never ceases to amaze me how God always seems to show up when we need him most.'

My friend responded that she had been reading a biography of Oswald Chambers and was struck by the lyrics of a song she'd never heard before – Chambers' favourite hymn. Intrigued, she went online to see if she could find a recording of it. As she listened to the music, the words spoke to her with even greater force. As she often does when finding wonderful things, she simply texted me a link to the song, with no further explanation.

The texted link displayed the photo of a young woman, and the singer's name. Coming from my friend, I knew the link would be good, so I clicked on it. The music started, with a melody unknown to me. But as the beautiful female voice began to sing, I recognised the lyrics – 'O Love That Will Not Let Me Go.'

I wept with profuse tears of joy, as I realised yet again the powerful love that the Creator of All has for me – not only embedded within the powerful words of this old hymn, but in the mysterious, invisible strings He must have pulled to bring about this incredible synchrony: of my saving the song's lyrics years before, then finding it mixed in the stack of sadness, rescuing it to my kitchen, a friend reading about the favourite hymn of a man who lived a century ago, and being so struck by the song she looked for it online, and finally, inviting me to hear the song myself.

An Unrelenting Love

Only a God who holds the vast universe in the palm of His hand, and who has infinite love for a tiny, flawed being such as I, ever could – ever would – pull off such a miraculous wonder as this.

Blowing my Mind

Adah Christabel

As I stood by my stove, on this 17th day of August 2023, waiting for the milk tea I was bringing to boil to rise, the Holy Spirit led me to my tiny kitchen window. My house is made out of mud. Initially, I had no desire, nor idea that I would live in it when I had it constructed.

My eyes settled on three young learners who attended our church fellowship, Joppa House of Worship. They were headed towards our little chapel, wearing their school uniforms. Emmanuel, Marcela and Tabitha had grown fond of me, and addressed me as Mum. Whenever they were sent home from school for anything, they would come straight to the sanctuary. They all came from vulnerable, humble homes.

What surprised me this morning was that they were headed to the chapel, instead of coming to the house. Then I heard a very clear voice. 'They have arrived!'

Startled, I asked, 'Who?'

'Students of Adornment Christian School!' came the prompt answer.

Confused, I went to them, and asked them to tell their parents to come to the sanctuary the following Friday so I could inform them that we were beginning a school. We had six learners who attended Joppa, and so I was confident that we would pull off a free school in my 12-foot by 12-foot gazebo.

Come the 25th of August, when I expected a maximum of five parents (two of the learners are siblings), I was bombarded by nineteen parents who proudly narrated how word got to them that I was starting a

Blowing my Mind

free school. If I thought those were many, by 29th August, the admission day, we had admitted 65 learners, and found 3 untrained teachers. Overwhelmed, I decided to send the rest of the parents away.

The following day the sanctuary was flooded with learners of all ages, with makeshift classes all over the compound. That was the humble beginning of Adornment Christian School. At the end of that school term, on 24th October, we had 115 learners. By this point, my next door neighbour had leased out his home to us. The same month, God gave us an acre of land adjacent to the sanctuary. We serve porridge for breakfast and lunch daily. We have since grown to 155 learners with 11 teachers, six of whom are trained. A small number of parents and guardians support us with 10kgs of maize for porridge per term. The majority of learners come from families that cannot afford that.

I watch a miracle similar to the two fish with five loaves unfold at school on a daily basis. The Lord led me to read the testimony of George Müller, the German who served in England running an orphanage funded by faith. God said to me that Adornment International Ministries should be 100% faith-based. God provides everything, including salaries, in amazing ways. Each day we witness as He multiplies whatever we have.

He said to erect a dominant canopy over the school gate and write on it, "Adornment Christian School. A Planting of the LORD, for the display of His Splendour!" The canopy is almost ready; He has provided the $2000 USD miraculously. Indeed, God is faithful and able!

Many of our learners have been delivered and healed miraculously from chronic illnesses they suffered prior to joining this school. We give God all the glory and honour!

Indeed, God does not have favourites. Coming from a messed up past, I would never have expected God to put such a huge call upon my life. It all began in late 2021 when I asked God, 'What should I do to become as close to you as is humanly possible?' The response caught me off guard. A gentle voice answered in my spirit, 'Love, love.' I answered back that I did not know how to love, love, could He teach me?

He began to teach me to love people unconditionally, even those that seemed unloveable. As the year approached the end, and I enquired who I was in His service, I was informed audibly, 'I have approved you, I have appointed you, I have commissioned you!' The Lord would inform me, 'You are my apostle. Your call is Titus 1:1.'

Being doubtful, bearing in mind that I despised myself, I pushed further and asked, 'What is my assignment, Lord?'

The answer was prompt. 'Your assignment is Love, for love is the excellent way!' The Lord would continue to teach me and reveal to me unsearchable things. He went on to tell me, 'I will blow your mind.'

Indeed, what the Lord is doing in me, through me and with me is mind-blowing! Late November 2024, I was preparing traditional vegetables in the gazebo, sharing with an acquaintance, when I received a call.

'I have been trying to find your contact all day. I am a gender-based violence officer at the county hospital. We have a desperate situation with a teen who is due anytime, through incest. We are requesting if you can accommodate her as we try to convince her to keep the baby, because the family has threatened to kill it to avoid disaster in the family. They believe the baby is a bad omen and hence should not be allowed to live!'

'Absolutely!' I responded. Adornment International Ministries is based on Isaiah 61:1-3.

Blowing my Mind

I did my best to convince the girl, and her mother, to keep the baby and continue with school while living with me. The response was always a resounding no. They both preferred to remain in the family rather than walk away because of little Precious, who arrived on 16 January 2025 at 10:30am and was thrust into my arms instantly. She was so tiny, and the doctor's advice was far from encouraging. 'If the cold touches her, she will be gone.' Minutes later, I left the hospital, without a penny, but with my petite bundle of joy. The Lord would blow my mind as He provided the expensive daily can of formula miraculously for baby Precious. Needless to say, no cold touched her, she is a very healthy and active baby, six months now and growing stronger each day. Indeed, as the Lord told me at the start of the year, through a song He gave me, 'I have given you favour and laughter!' Becoming a mother again at 59 years of age is the most joyful and precious thing the Lord has done for me; my mind is blown. Truly, those who wait on the Lord will renew their strength.

As I was still reeling from the miracle of Precious, the Lord revisited me, to remind me of His instruction over a decade ago that I should build a traditional wood oven for baking bread.

I took it upon myself to build the oven in Busia, the town I believed had the necessary number of consumers. I was relying on logic, knowing that many there earn a living through employment, hence their ability to purchase and thus grow the bakery. How wrong was I! We recently moved the oven to the village, and it's amazing how this small venture, 'Mustard Seed Craftery', is transforming families in this village where before the majority of fathers returned home late at night. Now it's almost like a competition to stop by at our temporary structure made out of mud to take home what is available on our shelf.

It is evident now that, when God said to me He had planted me as His light in this village, dubbed 'the village of fools', His plan was that His light will shine through me, for His glory to be seen through this ministry. It is extremely humbling to watch God feed us on a daily basis and pay salaries. At the end of each day, my mind is blown, just as He promised me.

A Lost Child Before Being Found

Yen Daly

I have decided to follow Jesus, no turning back.

The words fell awkwardly from Maigo's mouth. Whispered, empty. Certainly lost in the declarations around her. Swaying off-beat, she glanced around at closed eyes and raised hands. Faces furrowed in great concentration, or smiling, or blank, or hidden, bowed in chests. On the stage, four singers mirrored the audience, shifting their weight to the rhythm of an out-of-time band. Despite having microphones, they couldn't really be heard. But it didn't matter. The voices around her carried the melody in the large, boomy auditorium.

I have decided.

It was the weirdest rock concert she'd ever attended, but she felt right in her choice to have come. Next to her, hands in his pockets, was the latest boyfriend. Sure, she had spurned dating and the opposite sex only a few months earlier. But she found herself, yet again, giving in to the attention of an interested gaze. The heart wants what the heart wants, right? And what an insatiable master it is. He liked her. Somebody liked her. That meant something, right? And it's not like he was asking her to convert to his religion or something.

'As you know, I'm a Christian.'

'That doesn't matter.'

'Well…I suppose it matters to me.'

They played at adulthood, sipping coffee and pretending to like it. He had wanted to talk, after a couple of months of daily texting, hanging out, and then these last few weeks of stealing kisses.

'The purpose of dating...' He looked up apologetically. '...for a Christian, I mean – is marriage.'

Maigo blew gently over milk foam.

He continued, 'And I want a partner who'll be able to help me grow in my faith.'

A sip.

'And if I feel like that's not happening in our relationship, then I might have to break up with you.'

A scalded tongue.

Maigo lowered her mug slowly, her eyes glancing at the occupied tables around them. She was pretty good with words, but for some reason it was like he was speaking an altogether different language. 'I might have to break up with you.' Okay, so he wasn't breaking up with her – at least, not now, not yet. Breathing resumed. 'I want somebody to help me grow in my faith.' Grow in something. That's understandable. Understood. Growing is good.

In faith?

Faith.

She felt the boundary of her understanding. She could tell it was weighty. Important. Enough for the twenty-year-old boy in front of her to explain he would not need to see her naked, as nice as that would be, and he would be willing to leave her if she didn't support it, help it. This faith. A familiar tightening took over her chest. How was she supposed to support it, help it, if she didn't even know what it was?

Bodies, desire – this was the language of their peers. One she had practised and gruellingly mastered. But she already knew he didn't talk like the other boys. Wasn't like the other boys. It's not that they were awful, no. No one was abusive. They were all actually quite sweet in their own way. But time and time again, it all ended the same way. Are you dating? Shrugs. Do you like each other? Shrugs, again. That ambivalence used to deliver such a kick. The distance, a code for deep care and can't live without you. But at the end of the day, it somehow always ended the same, with her naked and in hiding.

Marriage was also glaringly absent from the lexicon of other boys she had dated. And definitely not anything she had wanted or aspired to. Sex. Get good at sex. Don't get too serious too early, or you'll miss out. On life. On real living. Why should it be taboo? Sexual freedom is independence, it's emancipation. True, she often thought.

But why does it hurt sometimes?

You're getting too involved, don't get too attached. It's okay, you're mutually using each other. But after letting yet another body in, while keeping emotions, attachments, commitments out, she couldn't help feeling like the used condoms tossed away at the end of those messy grasps for belonging, for acceptance. Maybe even love.

Tossed aside and thrown away. Thrown around. I throw myself around. Waiting to be caught. Any arms'll do.

Follow Jesus

Sitting in sweet smoke machine air, Maigo was again lost in translation. What was this preacher? – speaker? – priest? What was he saying? Some around her were taking notes, opening the smallest Bibles she'd seen. The only one she ever had the curiosity to read was the size of two bricks, and was being used to prop up her mother's Virgin Mary in their home foyer. The pictures in that one seemed childish. No pictures in these ones, it seemed.

She was ready to feel out of place. She had come here to support, to help. Not to belong. She was ready and equipped to defend any accusations of not believing in God, or her 'loose morals.' It didn't bother her in the slightest that everybody else knew the lyrics when the karaoke screen lagged behind, or when to stand up and sit down, or how to say Luke 15:24 as Luke fifteen verse twenty-four, and not like twenty-four hour time.

'If I feel like I'm not able to grow in my faith with you, I might have to leave you.'

He had said this, not quite knowing how to look at her. He was nervous, jittery, even pained. As if he wouldn't quite know how to leave her when it came to it. But, nevertheless, he did not avert his gaze. As if he, too, was ready. Ready to put something else before her, that did not wait for her to love him. Or require her to love him back. He didn't need her, the way those other boys did and then quickly didn't. The way she had needed all of them. The way she needed him.

He had something else. And she didn't. All these other people had something else. And she didn't. They stood by something, stood for something. They thought going after it, growing in it, was a much better pursuit than any race she was running. Heck, she realised, she hadn't really been running at all. But, floating. Aimlessly, endlessly. In open waters. While he, and all these other people, seemed anchored, docked at port.

No turning back

They were singing again. The preacher, speaker, priest got up, still without her making heads or tails about what he was saying. But some people really seemed to get it. They shuffled down the front, bowing heads, raising arms. Some were crying. Others placed hands gently on shoulders, with scrunched-up faces, murmuring into ears. This, apparently, was prayer.

She'd given up trying to guess the melody, her lips tightening, body hot. Tears found themselves on her face. What in the world? She was certain she wasn't sad or moved. Nor hurt or angry. Maybe mortified. There was Kleenex down the front, amidst the comfort and encouragement. She opted for her sleeves.

It is all ending. She glanced around, stopped by the gaze of the latest boyfriend.

'Was that okay?'

'Yeah, fine.'

'We're all getting dinner.'

'Maybe next time.'

She left that day, at the boundary of her understanding. It would take another couple of months of 'supporting and helping her boyfriend' until she could make sense of what the pastor was saying. But in time, she would come to learn about this Jesus, his Father, and his Spirit. She would go on to hypothesise it was the latter who caused her to cry that day. The start of scales falling from eyes, a phrase she'll learn from a much more famous story of someone else who had to reckon with a life-change.

In time, she would eventually find love, heal from what she thought was love, receive love. And not just from her latest boyfriend. He would give her a Bible inscribed with, "No matter what, this love will ALWAYS remain."

In time, she would find a place to dock and anchor.

But that day, she left. Not knowing what she wanted, what she was really seeking. Not knowing the meaning of faith. With no way of knowing that even after many years, she would still be asking what faith really means. That faith perhaps always starts at the boundary of understanding. She left that day, no decision, no Jesus, but knew somehow, there was no turning back.

The Graces of Dawn

Rory O'Donnell

Dawn is here. I watch from a secluded cliffside in the bush, having taken a pause from my wintry walk.

The sky slides from orange to yellow to an ocean of light blue. The sun's red light breaches the horizon, providing shivering trees a taste of its thawing power. I, too, await that power, huddled in shadow below the ridge as phantom needles stab my fingertips. My nose is numb, dripping like the dew. Will I get a chance at warmth?

The distant mountains, now a hazy blue, guard the mist pooling before them. The army of eucalypts stand in formation across the hills, their shadows curving with the crevices. They are unfazed by the chilly breeze in the sunlight. While I rub my hands together and bring my knees close, the sparrows freely flitter and chirp, jumping from tree to tree.

Still the sunlight has not heard my pleas. Why didn't it hear me as it did the birds?

Not even the smallest flower goes unnoticed by the sun. A purple flower with droplets dotting its exterior, housing a green speckled spider – even it's given care. A broken prickly pear defying gravity's decrees on the hillside is touched by the light too. The trees have come alive with their leaves cheering in gratitude.

As I sit, I realise the ridge is a sign of my apathy. I'm choosing its freezing shadow despite the Light yearning for me in all of nature, making visible the qualities of my Creator. Why am I not stepping out? I have no excuse. The sluggard I am now will find none of the Light's graces.

I take the path hidden in the grass, round the ridge, and come to behold the golden graces of the morning. I am warm. Like the eucalypts, the sparrows, the spider, I am seen. The Light had been awaiting me.

I stand in the embrace, relishing God's creation as though each sparrow, each flower, each spider was made to glorify Him, display His love, divinity and eternal power. I close my eyes in worship for a silent moment, then I continue my walk with the warmth and reminder of His Light in my heart.

Out of the Shadows

Kylie Gardiner

There wasn't a particular day when I lost my sister. It's not like she went on a walk and never came back. Her name was never on a missing person's list. It was more gradual than that. A slipping into adolescence, a rising paranoia, a fixation on never being enough. That's when I lost her. She went into a whole other world I couldn't understand.

I had few memories of my sister pre-adolescence. We weren't close sisters. There was a lot of pushing and shoving and name-calling. Both of us were guilty of that.

I've seen a photo of us smiling and holding hands, but I only remember how uncomfortable it was, and how we pulled apart as soon as the shot was taken. In Year 4, I was winded when a netball post fell on top of me. She came straight away to see if I was okay. It was the first time I remember her being concerned for my welfare.

At other times, she seemed to be devoid of emotion. She wasn't one to cry over a sad movie and seemed puzzled whenever I did. When Mum died, I never noticed a tear. But maybe that was just her way of coping.

I longed for a sister who would show you how to put on makeup. A sister to giggle with over your latest crush. A sister who looked out for you. Our neighbours had three girls. They taught me ballet positions and how to style hair. We would fall about laughing as we made up dances to the latest songs. I wished I had the bond those sisters had.

Michelle was about thirteen when she became obsessed with what other people thought of her, and she was always questioning me about her appearance. She would stand in front of the mirror, fake smiling and contorting her face to see if there were any wrinkles. I'd tell her a million times she looked fine, but she didn't seem to believe it. I thought it was vanity, but maybe it was self-consciousness and insecurity that trapped her.

She could still be good fun though, and her laugh was big and hearty. But her unpredictable behaviour overshadowed those moments. When friends or family came over, I'd be on tenterhooks. Would she make a scene? I ran around her fraying friendships, putting out spot fires. Continually apologising for her behaviour and making excuses for her. I worried people would believe the negative things she said about me. It was exhausting.

At thirteen, I became a Christian, and so did Michelle, but I found it very hard to pray for her. I was the older brother in the lost son parable. Resentful of her and thinking she deserved nothing good in her life. I found it hard to have any positive feeling towards her at all. Mum and Dad would try to normalise her behaviour and convince themselves that it was just a stage. She was a moody teenager but she would come good.

Michelle had a revolving door of boyfriends from the age of sixteen. An endless cycle of break-ups and back-togethers. I liked all of her boyfriends. They were nice guys, but a relationship with her was too volatile in the end.

One night after one of her 'episodes', I went for a drive. I felt like I couldn't cope with her anymore. When I finally went home, I walked into my bedroom, and it was completely trashed. The stereo I had bought with my first pay slip was in pieces. My dried flower arrangement was strewn everywhere. I knelt on the floor next to my bed, crying. *Why can't I have a sister who's normal?*

Then Mum came in. 'Why didn't you take Michelle to church? You know we want her to go to church.'

'Look at this bump on my head,' I pointed at the greying bruise above my eye. 'Look at my room. This is what she did to me.'

'Well, you must have provoked her.'

'I didn't provoke her! Stop saying that I provoke her.'

Mum was silent and left my bedroom.

I picked up the detachable speakers of my stereo and tried to put it back together. I didn't feel safe in my own room and asked to put a lock on my bedroom door, but Dad wouldn't let me.

Then things would settle down for a while. She would have a new boyfriend and wouldn't be home as much. I could breathe.

It was agonising to sit in church and hear the words in the Gospel of Matthew that urged reconciliation with your brother/sister. The words told me to prioritise reconciliation and forgiveness before offering a gift to God. I had to turn the other cheek, but I had no idea how to do that. It just felt impossible, and guilt trapped me.

Maybe it *was* my fault Michelle was like she was. Maybe Mum and Dad were right. Maybe I provoked her. I was no saint either. So I stopped yelling back at her. I disengaged physically and emotionally.

As soon as I finished university a friend asked me to be her housemate. I was earning some money now, so I could pay rent. I gathered my things and left. I told Mum I couldn't live with Michelle any longer. Mum admitted she found it hard too. The opportunity to leave home was an answer to prayer.

Eventually, I moved interstate for work. I was no longer the provocation, but her paranoid behaviour continued. There was a part of me that felt vindicated. It was finally obvious that it was not my fault. She behaved the same whether or not I was there.

A few years ago, my husband and I went back to my parents' place for Christmas. After having dinner out with an old friend, we arrived home to a smashed glass door and Dad sitting on the kitchen chair shaking. My husband recognised immediately that we had been dealing with a mental health issue; he had had experience of that in his own family. I phoned several mental health services but got nowhere. We went to the psych ward of the local hospital, but they told us to go to the police. The police told us to go to the psych ward. We threw up our hands. We felt defeated. How could we get her help?

Then Dad noticed she was saying strange things. She would read the newspaper and say all the articles were about her. She never stayed in one place for long because the police were always living next door to her. Every white van was surveillance stalking her. The police had put a bomb in her brain, and it would detonate any minute. Her paranoia increased to such an extent that Dad told his doctor what she was saying. The doctor immediately confirmed she had all the hallmarks of schizophrenia. She was put on antipsychotic medication. If she didn't take it, she would be put on a community treatment order. Fearing the police, she complied. Having a diagnosis was liberating for her, and for us. We finally had insight into the way her mind worked.

Something shifted in me. Slowly, I was letting go of resentment and hurt. I realised she had been living a tormented life too. In her mind, her thinking and behaviour were completely reasonable.

She was a different person on medication. I'd brace myself, but she didn't react angrily anymore. I didn't have to tiptoe around her. We could have a normal conversation. She asked me to pray for her, and this time I did, willingly. We could laugh and enjoy each other's company. She thanked me for the flowers I'd sent when she was ill. Something she would have never done before.

She'd been like a ball of wool in a tangled mess, but now we were winding it back together. But with this came an overwhelming sense of loss that it had taken forty-eight years for things to be mended. The resentment I'd felt toward her lifted. Slowly, forgiveness seeped into my prayers. Jesus took away my focus on the things that had hurt me over the years and enabled me to release that pain. My sister has never said sorry for her behaviour. She wouldn't have seen it as wrong because of the illness, but that doesn't matter. God has enabled me to forgive her and not require an apology in return. God's grace is powerful.

Now I could see things from her perspective. She had suffered a lifetime of loss too. Life would have been so different if she had been diagnosed as a teenager. So much pain could have been avoided. I was meeting my sister for the first time. She wasn't lost anymore. She had come home.

Rodrigo

Barbara McKay

'Your visit to the Brisbane Immigration Detention Centre has been approved.'

On reading this email, my face lights up like a sunflower lifted by God's grace in the morning light after days of bad weather. To say goodbye to a young man who was being deported from Australia after ten years in prison is a moment to treasure. *I may never see him again. I must say goodbye. He is like a son.*

My friends Pete and Gwyn drop me off at a demountable building where prison visitors were processed.

'No smiling, Barb,' they tease.

'How can I not smile?' How ridiculous. Asking me not to smile is like asking me not to sing the theme song when the Brisbane Lions win the AFL Grand Final.

I walk through the door.

Behind the desk, an officious woman looks up. She speaks sternly. 'Documentation?'

I open my iPhone and pass her the approval, hands shaking. 'Here is the reference number.'

'What do you have in your bag?'

'Two tiny sheep, made of clay, and some fabric with Australian designs. A gift.'

'Give them to me, please.'

She points to lockers on my right. 'Put your bag in that locker.'

Rodrigo

'Thank you.' I speak, voice trembling, but heart dancing.

So far, so good.

'Remove your shoes. Walk through the scanner. Stand here. Lift one leg. Now lift the other leg. Extend both arms.' She pats me from the armpit, all down my torso to my feet.

'Thank you. Now, walk through this door. Jenny will scan you.'

I conceal my smile.

'I need to frisk you with this wand.' Jenny says. *Why so many searches? Do they think a 75-year-old grandmother is smuggling contraband?*

Two minutes later, she points to the room with a dividing Perspex window.

Rodrigo sits opposite, his security guard behind him, arms folded, with a dead-pan look.

I walk into the room, and sit opposite my friend. Rodrigo beams a broad, mischievous smile like a beam of sunlight illuminating the coldness of this sombre space.

'*Hola, como estas, Mama,*' he says – 'Hello, how are you, Mama?'

My eyes light up. For the past year, I have written to this young man locked up in custody.

Rodrigo is a young Spanish man in his early forties, jailed by Australian Federal Police for drug trafficking. His shaved head and muscular build reveal his prison physique, likely a product of intense physical training. But instead of a hardened, guarded expression reflecting the harshness of a locked-up environment, his smile is as bright as the sunrise. His body reflects his survival but his face demonstrates hidden qualities of warmth, love and laughter.

Holding up a mobile phone gifted to him by an Anglican minister, he Facetimes his mother. He speaks in Spanish then flips his phone around to show me the picture.

I wave to his mum and blow kisses.

'What did she say? Can you translate?'

He giggles an infectious smile. 'She said, "Thank you for looking after my naughty boy."'

Our friendship began when I visited a country town to research family history – a town where my late husband had been the Methodist minister – a town where I lived when first married. On the Saturday I walked from the local caravan park to the Anglican op-shop. A young man with an accent greeted me.

'I need to buy a tea-towel. I'm camping,' I said. I finished the transaction and walked back to the camping ground.

The next day I decided to worship at the local Anglican church. This young man walked in and smiled. 'Can I sit next to you?'

'I don't know you.'

'Yes, you do. I met you at the op-shop yesterday.'

'Oh, yes.' I remembered. 'You can sit here.'

Whenever they announced a hymn, he quickly found the page, and handed the hymnbook to me.

At the end of the service, intrigue set in. I probed for further information. 'See those church people? I don't want to speak to them. I want to speak to you. What are you doing here?'

'I'm in a work-camp'.

Rodrigo

'What do you mean?'

'For good behaviour.'

I frowned, puzzled by his reply. He didn't mention the word 'prison' or 'jail' but he did mention the word 'custody'.

My brain clicked. 'Can I ask you what you did?' I spoke quietly in a cheeky voice.

'Google my name.'

At that moment, a bus pulled up. 'Gotta go.'

'What's your address? I'll write.'

His first letter revealed the secret of his optimism and joy. 'I became a Christian in the Capricornia Correctional Centre. I read *Word for Today* and *Soul Food.*'

As soon as I read those words, I knew, without a shadow of doubt, that God had brought Rodrigo into my life. Like sunshine in a dark place, my heart overflowed with love and tenderness for a young man who found employment with a drug cartel, was arrested and jailed with a long sentence.

Despite no training in pastoral care to prisoners, I wasn't deterred. Many years of experience had taught me how to disciple young Christians, how to provide fellowship and encouragement. For over a year, I wrote a weekly letter to his prison address, counting down the days until the night Border Force would deport him.

One day when I went to the local post office, I reached across the counter and handed the envelope to the post-master.

He smirked. 'Another letter for your toy-boy, eh!'

He placed a stamp on the envelope.

A 'toyboy'! I stood there speechless. *You have just poured mud all over my character.* It took everything in me not to explode. I was a spark away from combustion. I walked out. *Was he mocking me?* I chose to ignore his words, like water off a duck's back, knowing that my conscience was pure before God. As I walked to my car, my anger simmered, but silence reigned.

Looking through that Perspex window on the day he is to fly home, I rejoice that Rodrigo will soon be free. His smile radiates – warm, like sunlight breaking through after years spent in the darkness of a prison cell.

Speaking in clear English, he speaks sincerely. 'Thank you, Mama, for everything you have done for me…for being such a blessing in my life. I know it is God who gives you all that energy.'

The guard taps Rodrigo on the shoulder 'Five more minutes.'

We ignore him.

'How shall we close this visit?' I ask. 'Why don't you read Psalm 91?'

Picking up his phone, he searches for this beautiful psalm. He speaks clearly, finishes reading and looks at me.

'Why don't we pray?' I suggest.

Bowing our heads, we lift our voices in thanks to the living God, thanking Him for the fellowship we both knew since that first meeting. I wave goodbye, and he blows kisses back at me through the Perspex window. God has united us and would walk with us through whatever lay ahead.

The apostle Paul spoke to young Timothy and said, 'Onesiphorus often refreshed me and was not ashamed of my chains'. Jesus was a chain-breaker, bringing freedom and I am not ashamed to follow God's prompting in being a mentor to Rodrigo.

Rodrigo

July 2025

    Rodrigo returned to his own country. Within 24 hours of arrival, he faced the drug lords, explained his Christian faith, and asked to be released from their employment. My fellowship with him continues.

The Lion

Simone Field

Tick-tick-tick went my indicator as I slowly turned the corner. I was patiently waiting in the kiss-and-ride queue outside my daughter's school, while keeping an eye on my three-year-old in the back, fast asleep in his car-seat. Kindy sure did knock him out. Since he had started, he always had a nap on the way home. My heart softened as I looked at him sleeping, his sweet lips puckered, his eyelashes resting on his soft cheeks.

My gaze moved to my little girl coming up the path, looking oddly grown up in her school pinafore, hefting her school bag, which was more than half her size, behind her. She walked towards the car and opened the door with the duty teacher's help.

'Hi Mum,' my school-weary six-year-old said, as she climbed into the car. She settled her bag at her feet and conscientiously buckled herself into her booster seat.

'Hi chicken, how was your day?' I ask, reaching back to pass her a cut-up apple for the ride home.

'It was okay,' she said half-heartedly, toying with the apple.

'Just okay?'

'Yeah, Lila had to go home, so it was a bit boring.'

Lila was her best friend. The two were always giggling and playing together, so I could see how she would find a day without her not as interesting as usual.

'Ah, I see. I hope she's okay.' I spoke absently while indicating right to pull out into the traffic.

The Lion

In my head I was running through my usual evening dance. Get the kids home, wake up three-year-old, do home reading with the six-year-old, cook dinner (what will we have tonight?), fold the laundry and then put kids to bed…

'I dunno, she fell on the floor and started moving all funny. The teacher ran to her real quick, but then, I dunno, she just went home, I guess.' She started munching the apple, so I let the conversation dwindle.

Fell on the floor, moving funny. That didn't sound good. I made a mental note to call her mum at some point in the evening routine. At home I sent a quick text, 'All good? C told me L wasn't feeling well?' At the sound of the text whooshing its way across the suburbs, I quickly got side-tracked with the bustle of household machinations.

It wasn't until a few hours later, when dinner had been eaten, baths had been given, stories read and blankets tucked in that I thought to check my phone. The message was unread. Something started to coil in my belly. A bad feeling, a sense of foreboding almost. I decided to call. Straight to voicemail. That was not normal.

I left a voicemail, asking if she was okay and if she needed anything. I went to bed later that night, still unsettled, and fell into a restless sleep.

On waking, I checked my phone and saw that my friend had seen my message, but had not replied. I started to worry. What if something bad had happened to her little girl? The scenarios that ran through my head ranged from a seizure, to a fainting spell, to meningitis. What had happened?

I conducted the morning routine on autopilot, worry for my friend and her daughter etching a furrow in my brow. As I was leaning over his high chair, my three-year-old reached for my face and tried to smooth my forehead with his chubby little hands. It startled me out of my introspection and back into the present moment.

'Sorry, sweetheart, Mummy's mind was a million miles away!' I said, grabbing a facecloth to wipe the Weetbix remnants off his hands and my forehead.

'What's the matter, Mum?' queried Miss six-year-old.

'I was just thinking about Lila. I hope she's okay,' I said, aiming for a light tone.

'Well, Mum, did you pray to Jesus?' she said, looking up at me in her innocence, the question evident in her little face.

Huh. I didn't remember praying. I had been worrying it over though. Over and over, if I was honest with myself. My mind had raced from one bad scenario to another, all without asking for heavenly help. I sighed, both bemused and surprised that it had taken so long for the penny to drop. Prayer was the only way to stop this cycle of unhelpful worry.

'You know what, how about we do that right now?' I suggested. A quick nod and my little girl bowed her head and started praying. 'Dear Jesus, my friend Lila fell over yesterday. Please help her feel better and let her come to school so my friend is there to play with me. Amen.'

I let my shoulders relax. It was probably nothing now that I had worried about it all night; best not to jump to conclusions. I let my mind switch off as I moved through the rest of the morning, dropping my daughter off to school and then heading to toddler library time.

The Lion

I was sitting up the back at the library, watching my son engage with the story being read by the librarian when I felt my phone vibrating 'bvvt, bvvt' inside my pocket. I quietly took my phone out and glanced down. It was Lila's mum, texting me back. I opened the text, reading quickly.

'Sorry. Couldn't text. Bad news. At the hospital, L had seizure at school, it's called an AVM, will text later.'

My stomach plummeted. It *was* bad news. So what to do now? Pick up that worry again? Or go to my knees in prayer? Prayer it was. I quietly sent my scattered thoughts in Jesus' direction, knowing that He would be gracious to understand what I was asking. I prayed like this off and on all day, every moment my heart turned towards them, praying.

Later that night I googled. What exactly was I praying for? AVM, I typed. I soon found out what it was and was glad I had prayed first. It was scary to read. It happens in the brain, I learnt, where the artery and veins get all tangled up and try to do the wrong job, essentially. It needed surgery to fix it. Brain surgery? I looked at my little girl, the same age, sitting happily on the couch and my heart broke.

So I went to my room and got down on my knees and prayed. 'Dear God, you know what is happening here, you know the structure of Lila's brain, you know every cell in her body. You knitted her together and you can repair a dropped stitch. Let Lila know your peace and your healing.'

As I prayed, deep stillness washed over me. A picture began to form in my mind. I was walking down a hospital corridor, the green floor ahead of me, the walls white and sterile, the wooden hand rails on the sides. I turned right through an open door into a room and there was a hospital bed, off to the left-hand side as I entered, and Lila was sitting up on the bed.

Then I had to step back, because in the room was a large, golden lion. It was majestic. Regal, soft and scary at the same time. It was pacing slowly back and forth, in between the door to the room and the bed where Lila sat peacefully. The lion stopped, blinked at me and sat down firmly in front of her. I had the strongest sense wash over me in that moment. I knew Lila would be okay. The Lion of the tribe of Judah was watching over her, protecting her, guarding her life.

I slept soundly that night.

The next morning my friend messaged, 'Can you come in to the hospital? L wants to see C before her surgery'.

'Of course.'

An hour later, we entered the hospital ward. As the double doors whooshed open, I saw a hospital corridor, the green floor, the sterile, white walls, the wooden hand rails on the sides. I looked for the room number, found it, turned right through an open door into a room and there was a hospital bed, off to the left-hand side as I entered, and Lila was sitting up on the bed. A wave of goosebumps danced across my flesh. I felt a presence in the room, an otherworldly presence, a holy presence, confirming what I had received in prayer. Lila would be okay.

I shared my vision with my friend and the four of us gathered in that hospital room and we prayed and we gave thanks and we prayed some more.

Through brain surgery, recovery and many years of schooling, Lila is still fine. She is a super smart teenager now, attending a program for gifted and talented people that she was selected for.

So many years later it still remains one of the best memories I have of my daughter's primary schooling. We prayed, we witnessed the Lion in action and we can tell of His goodness for the rest of our days.

Isn't it time you told your story?

Over the years, a great many people have had their stories published, and many have been recognised as category winners. Do you have a story of faith and testimony? Will 2026 be the year you tell your story?

For the possibility of being published or winning a prize, please send us your true stories in one of these categories:

Open Category

maximum 1500 words

Short Category

maximum 500 words

Submission details, rules and writing resources can be found on our website:

https://storiesoflife.net

Have you written a book?
Not sure how to get it published?
Worried it will cost a fortune?
Not a problem.

Helping writers to become authors

info@immortalise.com.au

www.immortalise.com.au

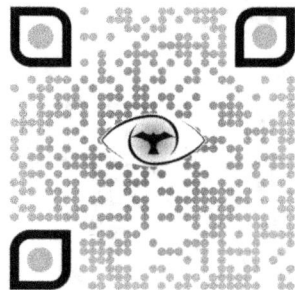

www.ingramcontent.com/pod-product-compliance
Lightning Source LLC
Chambersburg PA
CBHW071242070526
44583CB00017B/2298